THIS
IS
STRATEGY

THIS IS STRATEGY

Make Better Plans

SETH GODIN

AUTHORS EQUITY

Do You Zoom, Inc.

Authors Equity
1123 Broadway, Suite 1008
New York, New York 10010

Find out more at:
seths.blog/tis

First published in the United States of America by Authors Equity 2024
www.authorsequity.com

Most Authors Equity books are available at a discount when purchased in quantity for sales promotions or corporate use. Special editions, which include personalized covers, excerpts, and corporate imprints, can be created when purchased in large quantities. For more information, please email info@authorsequity.com.

Library of Congress Control Number: 2024942104
Paperback ISBN 979-8-893-31016-0
Ebook ISBN 979-8-893-31030-6

Printed in the United States of America
First printing

Traction is progress.

Help others get to where they're going.

Big problems require small solutions.

The work is easier if you can see where you're headed.

Change creates tension.

Better is possible.

Charles Wilson has a problem. He's one of the great pianists of his generation, inspiring people as he performs around the world. As the sole artist, composer, impresario, fan manager, COO and entrepreneur behind the persona of BLKBOK, he has too many options and not enough time. Being dedicated and skilled isn't enough–he needs to figure out how to increase his impact, build a sustainable career and not burn out along the way.

The Secretary of State has a problem as well. The US State Department is one of the largest organizations in the world, with countless staff and a huge budget. How to put them to work to make the desired impact in more than 150 countries?

Kristin Hatcher is doing essential work to deal with sexual violence, particularly on college campuses. While the urgency of her cause is clear, finding the traction to raise money and put it to work is an ongoing challenge, far more difficult than it should be.

Jesse Cole, founder and owner of the Savannah Bananas, had a problem. His remarkable idea was constrained by an existing system. Now, he is finding ever more success in bringing his wacky baseball jamboree to stadiums across the country. He recently made important decisions that freed the team from where they were stuck, and the options in front of them are multiplying.

When organizations large and small ask me about marketing problems, I often respond by saying, "you probably need a strategy first." But what's that? Strategy is difficult to see and not easy to talk about, because it happens over time.

To find a better strategy, we need to be prepared to walk away from the one we've defaulted into. When technology shifted, Nintendo stopped making playing cards and built a video game company. And yet, when the telephone arrived, Western Union decided to simply make better telegrams.

The world is shifting, faster than ever, creating opportunities and problems every day. This is our chance to make a better plan and to create a bigger impact with our work. This is strategy.

Perhaps you can't see it (yet).

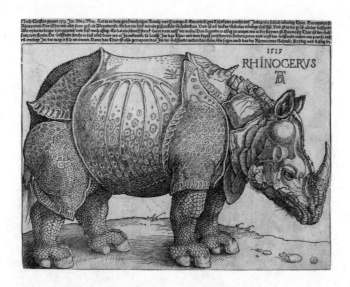

Most books on strategy are for corporate MBAs or West Point generals.

This is for you. For someone who wants to make things better.

My narrative is recursive and elliptical, circling back on itself as it seeks to help you see how time, games, systems, and empathy dance together to make our world. And once you see it, you can't unsee it.

About five hundred years ago, Albrecht Dürer made a poster of a rhinoceros, a creature that almost no one in Europe had ever seen in person. Each detail is finely rendered, but not quite right. But if you look at it for a while, the essence of a rhino comes through.

Strategy is often an unseen option, apparently too sophisticated, expensive, or elitist for most of us. But once we see it, our next steps become clear. We have what we need to make better plans.

Strategy is the soil, the seed, and the gardener working together over time. Strategy is our chance to make an impact.

As you work through this manifesto, it's okay to skip the parts that don't resonate (yet). Jump ahead, then loop back.

Stick with it. Discuss the parts that don't match what you're doing right now, and more importantly, the parts you don't want to be true.

Thanks for doing the work.

How to Use This Book: Find the others and ask the questions

I've workshopped the ideas in this book with people around the world, and we've discovered two simple ways to transform your relationship with strategy.

The first: Find three or four other people and start a group, in person or in Zoom. Meet once a week and make assertions, highlighting your fears and sharing your path. Surprisingly quickly, you'll notice that you're shifting your strategy.

The second: Use the questions, lists, and challenges in this book as prompts for claude.ai. Claude is a powerful AI that can take your prompt and personalize it for your project, challenging you to think about strategy in new ways.

Every riff here is numbered, to make it easy to refer to sections worth discussing, regardless of what format your colleagues are using to engage with the book.

The system is always changing. It's up to us to change it for the better.

1. STRATEGY IS A PHILOSOPHY OF BECOMING

Who will we become,
who will we be of service to,
and who will they help others to become
This is strategy.

A strategy isn't a map—it's a compass. Strategy is a better plan.

It's the hard work of choosing what to do today to make tomorrow better.

This is the point. This is at the heart of our work and the challenge of our days.

Toward better.

2. FOUR THREADS, WOVEN TOGETHER

Time, games, empathy and systems. They're everywhere we look, and easy to ignore.

Each supports and is supported by the other three. Throughout this project, we'll be shifting from one to the other, building up to a fuller, actionable understanding of how strategy works.

Time, because strategy plays out over time in the way a garden grows.

Games, because there are multiple players and different possible outcomes. Trees compete for light and only one grows to be the tallest, but all of them are part of the forest.

Empathy, because people don't see what you see or even want what you want. Plant your seeds in places where the conditions are right.

And Systems, because whenever we work together, a system is created. And that system often lasts far longer than we expect. The swamp isn't the same as the plains, but each is a complex web of interactions.

Each builds on the next in a never-ending braid.

3. WHAT DO PEOPLE WANT?

Once our basic needs for food, shelter and health are met, most people dance with three conflicting desires:

- Affiliation

- Status

- Freedom from fear

(We can probably add joy, wonder, thrills, satisfaction and other internal narratives, but for now let's focus on these three.)

Affiliation is community. Fitting in. Being liked. Affiliation is wearing the right fashion, using the correct salad fork and knowing the words to the song around the campfire.

Status is always relative. Who eats lunch first? Who's up and who's down?

And freedom from fear is an internal construct. Fear can be used as fuel, but it's more likely to be avoided.

Marketing works on these three principles. And systems all use them to maintain their structure.

If you want to understand why someone makes a choice, look for what people actually want, not only the proxies and substitutes they say they want.

4. THE NON-STRATEGY OF "TAKE WHAT YOU CAN GET"

"You can pick anyone. I'm anyone."

Hustle for attention. Do a very good job. Play it safe and follow the leader.

This is a non-strategy. The non-strategy of doing what we were told, of fitting in and settling. This is the non-strategy that comes from not thinking about strategy.

The number on the car's speedometer isn't always an indication of how fast you're getting to where you're going.

You might, after all, be driving in circles, really quickly.

We can do better.

I can't tell you what your strategy should be, but I know that you need one.

5. AWAITING INSTRUCTIONS

"What happens next?" is a different question from, "What will I do now?"

The easy out is to simply react to events and follow the checklist. Our freedom and agency demand we take a different path, though. Our work begins by finding a strategy and creating a different future.

There are choices to be made.

Stay put or move to another town... Stick around the firm to make partner or start your own practice... List your work on Upwork or Etsy or build your own store... put your music on vinyl or Spotify... raise your prices or lower them... open a new store or close the wholesale division... Go to a famous college at great expense or get a great education at a state school... have a traditional wedding or elope... start a blog or a podcast... Merge with a competitor or sell the business.

Too many choices, too many options.

Confronted with so much choice, it's tempting to simply do your job. To pretend that it's up to someone else, and to put your head down and follow instructions.

Don't surrender your agency and revert to the numbing day-to-day grind of compliance. You can make things better.

6. THE ELEGANT PATH IS THE MOST USEFUL WAY FORWARD

My neighbor is a barefoot runner. He glides without apparent effort. He's certainly not trying harder than anyone else out there on the track, but he's going faster, with less discomfort. Ten miles later and he's still fresh.

Elegance is simplicity, efficiency, and effectiveness. It's not only a solution that gets a result. It's arguably a *better* solution—the least complex and clearest way forward. An elegant strategy offers leverage in service of the change we seek. While it might seem effortless in execution, creating the method requires insight and care.

Elegant paths often seem roundabout at first, but they put systems to work for us, instead of against us. They require intent and discipline, and reward us with resilience and efficiency.

Our elegant strategy reduces waste. We avoid dead ends and save energy, time, and materials as well. And an elegant strategy is beautiful. We know in our bones that we're aligned with the systems and resources around us, doing the right thing in the right way. Pretending we don't need a strategy isn't nearly as useful as digging deep to find an elegant one.

Elegant strategies *use* systems. Even when they set out to change the system, they don't fight it directly but use the system as a tool to change the system.

This approach only gets better over time. The word spreads horizontally. Trust grows. Engagements lead to more engagements.

Each node in the system we engage with will make a choice about how to allocate attention and effort. Our project needs to be accepted by people who have the power to choose—and our job is to create the conditions for that to happen.

7. NOT ALL ELEGANT STRATEGIES ARE THE SAME

But many of them fall into similar buckets. Systems respond to strategies, and elegant strategies give us leverage.

Three things to focus on:

- **The strategy gets better as you grow.** Anyone can sprint, but elegant strategies are something that you can maintain.

- **Systemic advantage defeats heroic effort.** Heroic effort is thrilling, but long-term elegant strategies rarely require miracles on a daily basis.

- **They're simple to explain and difficult to stick to.** Over time, the pressures to vary from the elegant strategy increases—a thousand little compromises that eventually lead to mediocrity.

8. SYSTEMS ARE UNSEEN AND PERSISTENT

Strategy builds systems, but it depends on them as well.

Every successful system serves a purpose.

It might not be the purpose it says it serves, and it might not seem to make sense, but if the system sticks around, that's because the system is delivering on a promise.

It's difficult to strategize and make a difference if you don't understand the systems that are working to keep things as they are.

9. WE LIVE IN THE SOLAR SYSTEM

It may be worth taking a moment to think about a system where there is clearly no one in charge.

Earth, Jupiter, moons, and a million asteroids and meteors—they're all in a system with a star at the center of it.

It's held together by gravity, an invisible force that quietly and relentlessly controls the path of the planets. At the same time, the planets influence each other, and in a small way, the sun.

When a foreign interstellar object intrudes on our solar system, it either passes through or is captured by our system and becomes part of it.

If parts of the system are unseen, that doesn't mean they don't exist. As they say, gravity isn't just a good idea—it's the law.

10. SYSTEMS DELIVER VALUE

How did our culture evolve to have systems at the center of so much of what we do? There are three reasons:

Coordinated human effort creates productivity and value. When we work together, we get far more done. A doctor without drugs, hospitals, or a team isn't very effective. And a farmer can't feed anyone without tools, markets, and seeds.

People are rarely rational. Even when we want the same things, we don't always agree about how to get them. Systems adjudicate these disagreements and allow us to move forward even if we're not in sync.

Consistency is worthwhile, and slack and persistence of information permit this. If someone doesn't show up for their shift, or isn't operating at full speed, the system acts as a bridge.

The power and leverage that systems create can also cause them to create undesirable side effects and impede useful innovation.

11. THE BUILDINGS OR THE ROADS?

Stewart Brand points out that if you look at a map of Boston from 1924 and compare it to one from 2024, almost every building has changed over the last century. And yet few of the major roadways have.

It's far easier to renovate or replace a building than it is to reroute a road.

Systems have nodes (buildings) and connections (roads). Those roads have conventions that we all need to understand to stay safe.

Buildings (and people) get replaced all the time. Roadways (and the rules of systems) fight like crazy to stay the way they are.

12. THE UNSEEN ASSISTANT (AND THE MYSTERIOUS VANDAL)

Better waves make better surfers.

A useful skill in surfing is picking the right place and time to go surfing. The systems in our lives are like waves, making our work easier or more difficult.

Working *with* a system is like having an assistant, eager and skilled, always making your work better. But working *against* a system can feel like someone is intentionally harming your project.

When Michelin rolled out the puncture-proof tire, they were sure they had a billion-dollar innovation. It was better for drivers, car manufacturers, and the industry.

A few years later, the project was dead. Ron Adner explains that because the local tire shops, garages, and repair depots would need arduous training and new equipment, they hadn't eagerly participated in the early days of the project, and Michelin had largely ignored them.

As a result of this missing link, customers discovered that they had a great deal of trouble getting their tires serviced, and were often pushed to buy normal tires to replace their worn or damaged no-flat tires. Frustrated customers complained, and some even sued the car companies.

While it's easy to point the finger at the selfish car mechanics, the truth is that the vandal was the system—the resilient automobile industrial complex that would rather not change quickly.

13. CAN YOU SEE THE RIVER?

A river is more than water. There's water in a lake, too.

The essence of the river is the current. Paddling upstream is more difficult than going downstream. A snapshot shows you the water, but not its motion, not the relentless force as the water moves from here to there. *The river flows.*

If you want to change the course of a river, you can try to build a dam, but those are expensive and can fail.

The alternative is to dig a small channel that helps a river to go where it was going anyway. When you make it easier for the current to flow, the current will respond.

A small channel quickly becomes a torrent, and then the river itself.

14. THE COLLECTIVE

Why do birds fly in formation? What makes a bird join in? It turns out that the lead bird doesn't stay in the lead the entire time. The flock rotates. The collective evolved to find an efficient system for travel.

It works with people too. Any time that a person can benefit from engaging with a community, a system will evolve.

Most of us don't walk to the stream to fetch the day's water. Instead, we're happy to pay a small fee to get water from a pipe, which comes from a treatment plant, which is part of the city's infrastructure.

We don't try to persuade every person we meet of our status and knowledge. Instead, we paid (with time and money) to engage with an educational institution that awarded us a certificate in exchange.

And even if we spend our days working as a soloist, we're not alone. We're part of a collective or an industry, a system to take inputs and outputs and turn them into something of value for all participants.

Systems are everywhere humans engage to fill a need. Sometimes they persist longer than we'd like. Sometimes they move in directions we don't appreciate. Often, they're cultural, invisible, and hard to notice.

But systems define our lives.

15. SUCCESSFUL SYSTEMS

There are roles and rules, inputs and outputs, and rewards and punishments.

There are feedback loops, power dynamics, and hierarchies. Systems create the status quo and they defend it.

The system can be invisible, but the people involved in the system feel its pull and often understand that it has power. And effective systems create the outputs that define them.

There are giant, wealthy systems like college admissions, the military-industrial complex, or even capitalism, but there are tiny systems, like the dynamic in a particular neighborhood or the way the board of a non-profit makes decisions. Every family is a system as well.

We can't change capitalism. We can't even put a dent into it. But we can change the incentives of consumers, employees and investors by creating different cultural boundaries and status roles that operate within the larger system.

Systems can be as small as a nuclear family, deciding who gets a say in what's for dinner, and as large as a planet of 8 billion people, trying to deal with climate change.

Systems within systems. Turtles all the way down.

16. REAL LIFE ISN'T LEGO

Part of the appeal of LEGO for kids is that the pieces fit or they don't. A building goes together, comes apart, and can be put back together as it was.

This is very satisfying. It's also not very realistic.

Try taking apart a Hot Wheels car. It will take real skill to put it back together—the act of disassembling will deform its parts.

Even with the promise of interchangeable parts, there are million-dollar airplanes that will never fly again because they're missing a computer chip or a widget that's no longer available.

But the real truth of systems is that they're far more complex than even an airplane. Systems are more than built objects—they are the collisions between those objects and the natural world. They are the complex interactions of culture, of humans engaging with one another, of nature and chaos.

You can't step in the same river twice, because your footprint the first time turned the river into a different river. And it changed you as well.

17. TWO MYTHS ABOUT SYSTEMS

- You have unlimited power

- You have no power

We need a strategy because we can't simply order the system to follow our wishes. Part of our cultural mythos is that each of us has unlimited agency, if we're only willing to work hard enough, demand enough, and insist enough.

But systems are resilient and systems push back.

The power you have lies somewhere between infinity and zero.

It's possible that you've accepted whatever arrives, adopting the posture of a cog or (worse) a victim.

But we're not powerless. Individuals organizing others with persistence and generosity change the world, and do it every day. With the right strategy and resources, we can make an impact. Sometimes.

Buckminster Fuller taught us that to fundamentally change something, we must build a new system that makes the existing system obsolete.

Balance this temptation of building a new system with the insight from Carl Sagan that "If you wish to make an apple pie from scratch, you must first invent the universe."

It's unlikely anything we build is going to be built from scratch. But with time and focus, we can find the leverage to alter systems we care about.

18. BUILT, NATURAL, AND COMPLEX SYSTEMS

An airplane is a built system in which a designer and a contracting company create plans, sub-assemblies, and manuals, creating something they believe they have control over.

However, once a built system gets even a little bit complicated, unanticipated outputs begin to appear. The Tacoma Narrows Bridge collapsed because the engineers failed to account for harmonic resonances that would cause the entire bridge (which weighed millions of pounds) to sway and disintegrate once the wind was strong enough.

A corporate bureaucracy is a built system, but it's also a complex one. It acts in ways that no one, especially those in the HR department, could have predicted.

Complex systems create unexpected and unpredictable outputs. They're probabilistic and unstable, not deterministic the way we expect.

Decades ago, General Motors didn't set out to design mediocre, poorly built cars, but they did. Ford Motor Company didn't plan for the Pinto to explode and kill people.

There doesn't have to be a plan for there to be outputs. In fact, that's what usually happens.

19. WHAT MAKES A SYSTEM?

Human-built systems have elements in common. Generally, you'll find:

- **Boundaries**—they begin and end somewhere

- **Benefits**—people voluntarily engage with a system because they believe in the promises it makes

- **Bystanders**—often, people who don't want to be in the system are still involved in it

- **Information flows**—a shared language and expectations creates trust and efficiency

- **Stability**—the system offers its participants a reliable picture of the future

- **Protocols**—there are shorthands, processes, and methods of how things are done

- **Roles**—participants in the system seek or gain status and affiliation through their actions

- **Resilience and feedback loops**—when something disrupts the system, it works to push back and regain equilibrium

- **Convenience and efficiency**—even though systems aren't perfect, they offer participants outputs that encourage them to support it

- **Side effects**—every system also creates outputs that aren't ideal for non-participants or those that are part of it.

And so we find systems like:

- Big-time college sports

- Starbucks

- Religious practices

- The chocolate industry

- Your local volunteer fire department

- The community orchestra

- The dating scene in certain parts of Boise, Idaho

Decisions may feel as though they're voluntarily made. But the system exerts influence on each participant through each decision.

Each decision is the sum total of all the expectations, feedback loops, and invisible and visible rules that we adhere to.

20. THE PERSISTENCE OF SYSTEMS

We've lived with them so long they have become invisible, but systems are everywhere. Systems shift our perceptions and our actions, and they don't always offer us what we want or need. So why do they stick around?

Status quo—when people coordinate into networks and groups, our individual aversion to certain kinds of change is multiplied, and so the default becomes keeping things as they are.

Sunk costs—once we've invested our effort, money, and emotions into something, it's hard to let it go, even if it might not be what we need.

Interoperability—there are practical reasons for things to work in the way they do—connectors that connect, languages that are understood, and procedures that maximize efficiency. No one wants to buy a phone that doesn't support Bluetooth.

Status roles—the hierarchy benefits those that are at the top (who have power) and they work to maintain it. They also sell everyone else on the idea that the system is the best way for them to achieve status as well.

Affiliation—culture is "people like us do things like this." Humans find solace, satisfaction, and safety in community, and our desire for affiliation maintains existing systems.

It's a lot to undo. A more resilient and leveraged path is to work *with* systems instead of fighting them outright.

21. FROM FINE CHINA TO UNDERWATER HEADPHONES

Cultural systems evolve, layer by layer.

In 1759, Josiah Wedgwood used new production techniques to bring the world a refined, mass-produced set of china and pottery.

In 1843, Ada Lovelace did the groundbreaking work that informs computer programming to this day.

John Wanamaker pioneered the price tag in 1861.

By 1911, Frederick Taylor had published his ideas on scientific management, dramatically increasing productivity and quality.

In 1951, Lillian (Vernon) Hochberg began her direct mail campaigns.

The ubiquitous steel shipping container, first used in 1956, made shipping finished products around the world far more reliable and cheaper as well, enabling companies like Walmart to eventually transform retail.

The toll-free number, launched by AT&T in 1967, connected consumers directly to companies, allowing them to use credit cards, launched in 1950, to buy things directly.

Ethical email marketing, created by Yoyodyne in 1992, opened the door to electronic ordering, which was amplified dramatically by the adoption of web browsers a few years later.

And then Amazon wove it all together.

Which explains how I can buy a pair of Shokz underwater MP3 headphones online and get them delivered to my home the next day—for the equivalent of $2 in Wedgwood's time.

22. DUNCAN HINES (AND NINA ZAGAT)

Duncan Hines was a traveling print salesman, operating in the midwest of the United States a hundred years ago.

There were no health inspectors for restaurants, which meant that visiting a strange town and going out for dinner carried real risks. Food poisoning was common.

Duncan liked to eat, and with the automobile becoming more reliable, he traveled a lot as well.

Combining his printing expertise with his love for food, Duncan began to publish a travelers' restaurant guide. His focus was on places where a traveler could find a safe place to eat a decent meal.

The first year, he sent it out as a Christmas gift to a few hundred people. In the years that followed, demand for the guide grew, and he began to sell it.

Soon after that, restaurants inquired about being listed—the traffic and status that came from being listed was extremely valuable to them.

Hines offered restaurants a chance to be included: If they paid a fee, he'd send an inspector. If the business passed muster, they'd not only be listed but be given a sign to put up in front of the restaurant.

This status ratchet spread, and the food safety of restaurants around the country was transformed. His project improved the health of millions of people. It made him rich and famous, and ultimately led to the licensing deal that still has Duncan Hines' cake mix in every supermarket.

Several generations later, Nina and Tim Zagat, New York lawyers, put together a pocket-sized guide to restaurants in New York. They had a particular point of view: These were restaurants for people who went out for dinner a few times a week. Tapping friends and friends of friends to contribute reviews, the book listed thousands of restaurants with a unique, quotable style of short insights.

And they included three numerical ratings for each restaurant.

The result? Restaurants in New York, and then around the country, changed their businesses to score well in the guide.

DNA tests, passports, digital surveillance, rankings, membership lists, and SAT scores are all transformative because they surface data and turn it into information.

Information changes systems.

23. ALL DOGS ARE MIXED BREED DOGS

The only thing that makes a purebred so valuable is that an association labeled it.

The status conferred on breeders and owners of dogs that match the invented profiles of the AKC and other organizations drives them to commit to the system.

The end result is a health crisis due to inbreeding, together with a shelter system that often has trouble keeping up with puppies rejected or unsold by breeders.

There are almost a hundred million dogs in the United States, and every one of them is affected by a simple rule book of what sort of dog someone said they are.

24. U.S. NEWS CHANGED COLLEGE

U.S. News & World Report was a struggling weekly magazine, in third place behind *Time* and *Newsweek*.

To make ends meet, they put out a special report ranking colleges in the United States.

The first edition was fairly informal, based on limited data and some hunches.

But because it caught on and made a little money, they decided to reinvest and turn the guide into a business on its own.

They pushed back against resistance from college presidents, brought in various research modalities, and added countless variables. It's almost impossible to rank something as diverse as educational institutions, but they did it anyway.

As the rankings increased in visibility and acceptance, status was awarded (or lost) as a result. Universities started assigning staff members to look at the game, to understand the statistics, and to take action to move up the rankings.

Some of the side effects include:

- Schools dramatically increasing spending on sports facilities

- Scandals at schools like Columbia, caught cheating on their self-reported statistics

- Many schools shifting focus and curriculum and grading approaches in response to low rankings

- Other schools creating easy-to-fill-in applications for high-scoring students, simply so they could reject them and improve their metrics

By narrating, labeling, and publishing a hierarchy, an outsider changed a system that had been around since before the country was established.

25. WHERE'S THE METER?

Donella Meadows shared a story she heard from a researcher in Denmark. In 1973, they examined a suburban neighborhood of Amsterdam, where all the houses were very similar.

Some of the houses had their electric meter in the basement. Others had the meter in the entrance hall, where residents couldn't help but notice the power usage every time they entered or left their home.

All other things being equal (and they were), the houses with visible meters used one-third less electricity than their neighbors.

26. SEEING (AND CHANGING) THE CHOCOLATE SYSTEM

The farmers who grow chocolate are some of the lowest-paid workers anywhere. In Ghana and the Ivory Coast, two of the largest producers of chocolate, a commodity system grinds people down, pushing them into endless hard work, and not rewarding them for the taste, innovation, or quality of the chocolate they produce.

Commodity chocolate is cheap, and needs to be sold in volume to people who care more about the convenience, price, and social interactions than they do about the flavor or the impact of their choice.

There are several systems at work here: The corporate industrial complex, which pushes for scale, profitability, and stability. The government regulatory system, in which bureaucracies balance social good with pressures from industry as well as a desire for stability. And, of course, the marketing system, responding to consumers who prize convenience and promotion.

Turning Halloween into a cultural phenomenon benefits the largest producers of chocolate. It's not unusual for 15% of their annual sales to be associated with this single celebration. The key metrics for them are market share and profit, not flavor or sustainability.

In 2003, Dutch journalist Teun van de Keuken reported on slave labor in the commodity chocolate market. His initial plan was to use publicity to shame the government and large chocolate companies to change the system.

His frustration with the system led him to become a producer, and he founded Tony's Chocolonely (named this way because he was the lonely voice speaking out). Tony is now one of the largest chocolate makers in the Netherlands, with nearly 20% of the Dutch market. Their chocolate is fully vetted, from bean-to-bar, offering consumers a different story, a more delicious option, and a better way forward.

Shawn Askinosie took a similar path in the US, combining open book management, ethical sourcing, and dramatically higher wages for chocolate growers (it helps that it's more delicious chocolate as well). Shawn brought commitment and bravery to a new industry and as a result, changed the standard for how it should be done.

A third enterprise, Original Beans, seeing the possibilities in a new system, committed to pushing it further, making bars that are vetted, using profits to regenerate the landscape, and also embracing once-lost flavor profiles that some people happily pay extra for.

Neither Shawn nor Tony nor Original Beans is going to change Halloween. But the options they create put pressure on the system at every step. Governments are no longer easily persuaded that it's not possible to trace chocolate back to the producer. Retailers realize that they can make a profit year-round without pushing junk for a few weeks a year. And consumers in search of status and affiliation can engage with this new story, particularly when friends and colleagues highlight the options.

"Better" is a tricky goal. The system wants what it wants until leverage points are found that enable cultural shifts to happen over time.

Horizontal change is harder to see than brave leadership, but even more important

The movies need heroes. Corporations need CEOs. Inventions need inventors.

And yet, *culture* is the driver of most systems, and culture is the result of the interactions between and among people. Strategies stumble when they depend on someone with power dictating how things will occur.

If you want to grow a garden, you'll need to plant seeds, but it's the ecosystem and the climate that will determine what happens after that.

Our job is to find a plan and then create the conditions for our project to spread from person to person, within and across the systems that already exist.

27. SERIOUS GAMES

Getting your insulin dosage right is a game. Getting the farm bill passed in Congress is a game. Finding a job is a game as well.

You move, then the system (actually, someone in the system) makes a move in return. There's a competition—for attention, for resources, for slots—and there are outcomes.

Often, there are random elements as well. No one is a perfect game player, and no one wins every time.

Your body is a system. If you have diabetes, getting your insulin right is a challenge, because the system isn't optimized on its own for your health and well-being. Take too much and the system pushes you one way. Too little and the system pulls you in a different direction.

And the game of finding a job engages with a system, one that's defined by scarcity and opportunity. Each action the job seeker takes requires effort, and sometimes these actions over time turn into the job that they're looking for.

Serious games are all around us, whether we choose to play them or not.

28. THERE ARE GAMES IN EVERY STRATEGY

A game has the following elements: players, rules, scarcity, choices, feedback loops, and outcomes.

Calling the project a game gives us a chance to depersonalize our work, to be more flexible in our approach, and most of all just to talk about it. Smart people have studied games—from nuclear proliferation and public health to poker—and we can learn from them.

Here are a few things about games that are generally true:

• You don't have to enjoy the game for it to be a game.

- You're playing a game whether you realize it or not, and seeing the game helps you play it better.

- The outcome of a game often has little to do with how much you want to win.

- Everyone playing the game sees it differently.

- Some games are easy to quit, other games are forever.

- Not all players follow the same rules or have the same goals, even when playing the same game.

- No game stays the same for long, because playing the game changes the game.

- Short-term gains can lead to long-term losses, and vice versa.

- Sometimes the best way to win is to help others succeed.

- Large games are made of smaller games, all the way down.

- Most games are not fair, and some games cannot be won.

- The most valuable skills in one game may be useless in another.

- Some games become easier as you win, others more difficult.

- You don't always have to play the game you're offered.

- Multiplayer games sometimes conceal themselves as two-player games.

- We often spend more time figuring out how to win the game we're in instead of choosing which game to play in the first place.

---

29. WE ARE ALL TIME TRAVELERS

And we are all farmers.

The seeds you plant today won't grow for weeks or months.

The systems we support, the people we dance with, the ruckus we create—it's not for today, it's for tomorrow.

We're here, now, but we live in the future. We are making history.

If you could have tomorrow over again, would you do it differently?

30. SEEING TIME

Time is simply nature's way of making sure everything doesn't happen all at once.

The reason people have difficulty understanding the nature of evolution and the science of Darwin or even of compound interest is that we have trouble seeing time.

Perhaps we're here because of everything that happened in the past.

Or perhaps it's more useful to realize that the future is counting on us to create what comes next.

There's the world right outside our window, the world of here and now.

But we also remember yesterday. Who we were and what happened.

And we also know there is tomorrow. If we take action today, something will happen soon.

We can invest (or withdraw) from the days ahead. We can pay the price or enjoy the benefits of the work we do today.

Often, we go from yesterday to today as a bystander, floating on the currents of change. But when we are at our best, we actually create our future with intent. The future counts on us to make it better.

Strategy is the hard work of choosing what to do today to improve our tomorrow.

31. THERE IS A METHOD

Either we make the system or the system makes us.

Constructing a strategy connects our goals to our insight, amplified by our resources, and allows us to make a difference. Our blueprint is the actionable strategy we're committing to.

A series of 17 questions shines a light on the work to be done. It brings tomorrow forward to today, right here and right now, allowing us to articulate a strategy.

- Who are we here to serve?

- What is the change we seek to make?

- What are our resources?

- What is the genre we're working in?

- Who has done something like this before me?

- What systems are in play?

- Am I changing someone's status?

- Why would anyone voluntarily choose to be part of this work?

- What will they tell their colleagues?

- Who gains in status, affiliation and power by supporting this work?

- Will early support translate into more support later?

- Where is the network effect?

- What do I need to learn to make this work?

- Who do I need to work with?

- Where is the dip and when should I quit?

- What will I do if it doesn't work out?

- How much is enough?

These questions will make someone who wants to be a milkman, a movie star, or even a US Senator impatient. We've been seduced into seeking out jobs, but these questions challenge us to find a strategy, a way to prepare for the stepwise path to get from here to there. Too often, we pick a job we want to do and work backward to answer the questions, but that's arrogant and insulates us from the reality of the systems we need to dance with in order to reach the people we'd like to serve.

Get the strategy right and the jobs we do will be more fulfilling and easier to accomplish.

32. THE HEARTBREAK OF AN INTUITIVE STRATEGY

It's easy to fall in love with a dream. It might be the dream of opening a little bookstore, or of being a social media influencer. Perhaps it's a series of promotions at work, or the chance to organize a community to take action.

We've been taught to follow our passion, to do what we love and the success will follow.

Alas, it might be that our passion and intuitive instinct came from a system that doesn't actually support the work we seek to do or the change we seek to make. The rat doesn't know someone built the maze.

The challenge is that our passion and our love is probably based on an inkling of what we think is going to work. We subconsciously become aware of what's possible, and then focus and commit to a path, one that soon becomes our identity. If your passion is writing screenplays, it might be because you grew up in a world where there were movies—no one was born to win an Oscar four hundred years ago.

Plenty of kids in Cleveland dream of being a pro baseball player, yet few say that their passion is to grow up to be a blacksmith. We're not *born* with a specific passion, it is produced based on what we encounter and what's expected, even if we can't put the strategy into words.

It might be that our *actual* purpose is simply to be of use, to be productive and to make a difference. In other words, to have an elegant strategy. The specifics aren't nearly as important as the journey. Even if our project doesn't always succeed, it is the path for us to follow. It benefits us because the liminal state of seeking to get from here to there allows us to become truly alive. Life without a project fades to gray.

The hard work of developing a better, more resilient strategy begins with letting go of the assumptions and goals you might be holding on to right now. "Simplify, then add lightness," said Colin Chapman, the founder of Lotus Cars.

Simplify because the needless complexity we're stuck with was only created to insulate us from fear. And lightness because our agility increases resilience.

"Simple" doesn't mean that you're making a smaller impact or settling for less. It means choosing a strategy that puts you on the hook. It's a chance to be a meaningful specific, not a wandering generality. A strategy that's worth talking about and improving. A strategy that's easy to describe and difficult to stick with.

Falling in love with an outcome often prevents us from doing the work we're capable of contributing.

33. HIDING FROM A USEFUL STRATEGY

Once we clarify, simplify and commit, the useful strategy creates its own challenges.

What if it doesn't work? If we make promises and lean into a path that requires emotional labor, time, and effort, we're responsible. On the hook and with nowhere to hide. And any project worth doing might not work.

And what if it *does* work? Are we willing to let go of our status quo enough to embrace the possibility that we might make an impact? Are we ready to become whoever we will be if the strategy succeeds?

We often have more agency that we'd like to admit. Hiding is easy, but our project demands that we show up and make an impact.

As Michael Porter has pointed out, a strategy isn't a goal. And a strategy isn't a list of tasks. A strategy is the set of choices we make (and stick with) as we seek to compete. Hard choices are easy to hide from, since choices feel risky. And competition is challenging. It's easier to have a meeting about our mission statement than it is to get serious about choosing and persisting with a strategy.

34. LOW-HANGING FRUIT ISN'T

It's all been picked.

The easy, direct, obvious paths are unlikely to get you the results you're working so hard to obtain. In fact, these paths are probably a trap, part of a system that takes advantage of people who are looking for something convenient and apparently satisfying.

The best employers don't recruit at the placement office, and the most worthwhile projects aren't always obvious.

35. ROME WAS BUILT IN A DAY

Of course it wasn't finished in a day. It still isn't.

But as soon as the brothers announced that "This is Rome," there it was. Built, but incomplete.

After that, the work became the tireless, recursive, and repeated effort to improve the system and to grow the community that is Rome.

They started it in the right century, in the right place, with the right philosophy.

And then, each day, Rome got better.

Better, not done.

36. ONE TELEPHONE IS WORTHLESS

Alexander Graham Bell didn't invent the telephone.

He also didn't wire the world, or create 800 numbers, or come up with the smart phone.

What Bell did was build the Bell System. He published and licensed the protocol for local businesses to hook up their phone networks to the larger global network.

The breakthrough was in seeing the obvious fact that a telephone works far better if you can use it to call anyone else who has a telephone.

Over time, that means that every phone user has an incentive to work with the biggest system. Build a useful phone network and every phone user will eventually insist that the non-phone users they know go and get a phone.

And yet, even with the extraordinary advantages in speed, efficiency, and community that the phone brings, it took 75 years for a million people to have one. That's because networks used to be difficult and slow to build.

It only took Facebook 10 months to reach a million users. A hundred times faster than Bell took.

A few years later, Mr. Beast made a video that reached a million people in less than two days.

Few people reading this are working to build something as universal and game-changing as the telephone, but everyone reading this can benefit from understanding network effects, because they're everywhere, and with more impact and speed than Bell could have imagined.

37. THE DESERT ISLAND MYTHOLOGIES

There are two people on the island. Only you and me. And every interaction we have is right here, right now.

Except it's not that way.

Every person in your life is connected to someone else. To countless someone else's. Each decision we make is about our standing, our connections, and our community.

And in the real world, time looms large. The interactions we have today will change us for tomorrow and for the tomorrows after that.

It's not a dyad. And it's not simply about right now.

Everyone is in the room, and the room is here today and tomorrow as well.

It's a network. A network of community systems connected across time.

38. CITIES ARE CONTAGIOUS

Without people who have moved in from somewhere else, the city would only be as dense as the countryside.

Cities are connectors. When they work, it's because the others are there as well. The successful city persists because it's worth more to be part of it than to be apart from it.

And the metaphor is real: our project, the network effect, the movement, the connections—they are a city. Our city. A system that is part of other systems, with a chance to make a change happen.

We can create the conditions for it to thrive. No one wants to be hustled, but plenty of people are eager to be part of something that matters.

Change happens over time, but hastiness undermines an effective strategy.

39. ANALYZING THE LAST MOVE

When the deal falls apart, the team loses the game, or a partnership hits the rocks, it's easy to focus our energy on the most recent event.

"What if they had called a different play?"

This overlooks the real issue. It's the first move, or the fifth, that led to this problem, not what happened at the last moment.

Creating the conditions for success is a very different project than finding a heroic move that saves the day.

40. STRATEGY AND TACTICS

In 1968, the *Sunday Times* of London offered a cash reward to the first person who could singlehandedly sail around the world. They promised adventure, fame, and a trophy as well.

Where does strategy end and tactics begin?

The brave sailors who chose to commit to the race had countless decisions to make. What sort of boat? Should it be wood (easy to repair) or steel (unlikely to break in the first place)? What sort of electronics should they have, and what sort of backup systems? Should they even enter the race?

These strategic choices ended up determining the winner.

The tactics occurred after the race was on. Given a limited amount of time and few choices, what's the best option to support the strategy?

Tactics require skill in the moment and can consume us. Strategy is easy to skip, because we've trained our whole life for tactics.

Strategy is a philosophy, based on awareness of our goals and our perception of the systems around us. Tactics are the hard work we do to support our strategy. But great tactics don't help if the strategy is working against us.

Robin Knox-Johnston won that race around the world. His philosophy about boat maintenance made up for the mishaps he faced along the way. His strategy was correct, and the tactics were good enough to support it.

41. TOWARD A STRATEGIC PRACTICE

We manage to fill our days with activity, but how can we show up to make a difference?

There are three ways to put effort into a project:

• Chores and tasks

• Leverage

• Emotional labor

Chores and tasks are work we hire ourselves to do. This might be most or all of your day. Clearing your inbox, answering the phone, doing your job. Chores and tasks are all there is for workers in a factory. Sometimes they are satisfying, letting us off the hook, but they don't take us very far.

Leverage is the work we outsource. Outsourcing is far easier than it used to be, but challenges us to use our resources wisely. When we do the work that only we can do, we generate enough value to hire others to do the chores and tasks that they're willing to do.

And **emotional labor** is the work of change, decision-making, and strategy. It is the difficult work of embracing incompetence as we learn new skills, and the challenging work of seeing and then implementing real change. This is easy to avoid, which is one reason we spend so much time on chores and tasks.

Rembrandt, Andy Warhol, and Kehinde Wiley created impactful visual art. Each changed the culture and made a difference that will last. They built studios, hired craftspeople, and created more with a team than they could alone. They leveraged their skill by hiring others to contribute, sometimes even asking them to do the painting itself.

Each artist knew that there was work that only they could do. They set the style, signed the work, showed up for royalty or at Max's Kansas City, and were mindful of their public role. The paintings were the work of a team, but they produced the art.

And they each leaned into the emotional labor of decision-making. What's next? Who should be hired? What's good enough to ship?

We can choose where we provide leverage, or we can put as much time as we like into tasks or chores.

---

42. PROJECT WORK IS DIFFERENT

When you do a job, you do your job. Your boss decides.

Our life is a series of projects. It's not a job.

But projects are a choice, and our freedom gives us the chance to navigate systems and create meaningful change. That change always happens over time. Not right now, but bit by bit, move by move, day by day. Our work touches the market, and the market touches back. Our work influences one person and they influence someone else. We are not an event. We are choosing a path.

Strategy is a compass that helps us to take action when we're uncertain, to build networks when we're alone, and to persevere until the world we live in becomes the world we imagine.

43. YOU MIGHT NEED A STRATEGY TO

- Get into the college of your choice

- Find a new job

- Increase sales of your new product

- Decide where to live

- Get your neighbors to come to the local block party

- Pass the school board budget

- Get married without spending more than you should

- Change the bullying culture at work

- Help a new kid feel welcome

- Have enough savings to retire with

44. SLITHERING, WITH PATIENCE

Justin Kobylka is the most successful breeder of ball pythons in the world.

Before the internet, that wouldn't mean much. But because we're all connected, collectors can now share videos and trade via online marketplaces, and the system around breeding and selling snakes has been rebuilt from the ground up.

It went from being an oddball backyard hobby to a multi-million-dollar industry.

As a system matures, a small head start can lead to more assets, allowing investment, patient decisions, and the building of trust. The feedback loop amplifies small advantages. People want to buy from the market leader, giving that leader even more of an advantage.

Justin's company, Kinova Reptiles, has a perfect five-star rating on Morphmarket, the dominant sales platform in the category. His incubation facility is huge, spotless, and efficient. And most of all, his patient devotion to the craft permits him to evolve previously unseen varieties of snakes, some of which sell for more than $30,000 each. His strategy is clearly stated, and no one is likely to catch up.

The elegance in this approach is seen in how he dances with time.

The timing of growing in sync with the industry, transformed by the use of videos and online marketplaces.

The timing of investing in creating the conditions for the entire field to grow, with his company at the center.

And the timing of building the resources to do it even better tomorrow. He told Rebecca Griggs, "I've had offers of over a hundred thousand dollars on a snake, but the way I operate, it's important to keep those snakes for my future work. You actually lose money long-term if you sell the most amazing thing at the time."

He took a small head start and reinvested to turn it into a bigger lead. Now, buyers brag about the provenance of a snake. If Justin bred it, it's worth more.

His pioneering work, his spotless facility, and most of all his reputation keeps fueling more of the same.

45. PLANTS MAKE PEOPLE HAPPY

While still in her 20s, Eliza Blank quit her marketing job and opened the Sill, an online seller of house plants.

Ten years later, they have millions of dollars in annual sales, seventy employees, and several retail establishments.

The metaphor of tending and nurturing a plant isn't lost on Blank.

She started the Sill when the internet was reorganizing the system of finding, learning about, and buying plants. Without a storefront, she was able to put her very limited resources to work by hand-delivering plants throughout New York. As the word spread, she was able to invest in creating content (which brought new visitors and then customers to her site) and shipping across the country.

Her blueprint can't be the blueprint for the next competitor because the world keeps changing. One can copy the leader, but if the leader has deep roots and continues to plant new seeds, following will always be difficult.

46. SEATBELTS SAVE LIVES

Of course they do. It's obvious and easy to demonstrate. As a public health intervention, there are few that are cheaper, easier, and more effective.

More than 90% of drivers buckle up, which is required by law in the United States. But from 1968 to 1985, when seat belts were first required in cars but weren't mandatory, usage was under 10%.

While it's tempting to believe that once people saw the clear data about the safety of seat belts they began using them, that's not what happened.

The insurance companies were spending a fortune settling claims, and were pushing hard for car companies to be required to install passive restraints like air bags. One Secretary of Transportation passed a rule requiring it, then the next administration canceled the rule, then the next one reinstated it. Finally, the Supreme Court ordered the government to choose a consistent path.

At the time, the Secretary of Transportation was Elizabeth Dole. Serving under Ronald Reagan, she didn't want to be on the hook for ordering the car industry to do something it was lobbying against. So she ordered that unless more than half the states made seat belt use mandatory, she would order passive restraints installed in all new cars.

The car companies didn't want to pass on the considerable expense of passive restraints, and saw that altering their position to seat belt laws was a smaller shift to the system they were part of.

After Dole's ruling, it only took five years for more than 70% of the states to pass a law. The combined lobbying from car companies and insurance companies was irresistible to the states, who could point to the body of research as their motivation.

She created the conditions for opposing views to build a coalition that shifted the system.

Public health regulations are rarely a purely grassroots effort. Outcry helps, but persistently aligning the interests of forces in the system is critical. When divergent interests benefit from shifting the rules, progress is more likely to happen. Coordinated action is the only thing that changes the system.

Seat belts have saved more than 400,000 lives in the US since then.

47. AIRBNB WAS LOST

They got found in Austin, Texas.

The original idea of Airbnb was simple: People with an extra room or couch could offer it to a traveler for a night or two. It would save money and also build connections between strangers.

There are a lot of spare rooms in the world and a lot of travelers. But until both sides of the marketplace arrived, no one was going to use it—and in fact, no one was.

The founders of the site realized that the SXSW conference in Austin was a perfect smallest viable audience. Not only was there a shortage of hotel rooms, but the attendees at the conference were generally young, traveling solo, and adventurous. Even better, they were tech influencers, individuals who found status by sharing their discoveries with others.

The work to be done was straightforward: Find a few hundred people in Austin willing to give hosting a try.

Once they were able to enlist the hosts, they could bring the idea to an audience that was eager and ready for it. Over the next few days, hundreds of people, nodes in a critical system for the company, experienced Airbnb.

They tweeted, posted, and shared their experience. They didn't do this to help Airbnb—they did it because it helped them achieve their own goals.

And then the system they were part of did the rest of the work.

48. TWENTY-SEVEN EGG DISHES

Beryl Shereshewsky has nearly a million subscribers to her YouTube channel. It's not unusual for one of her videos to get more than 1,000 comments, all of them useful and generous.

Countless people want to be famous on YouTube, and nearly as many want to show off their cooking skills.

Beryl's approach, which is quite profitable and has earned her a show on PBS.com, sees and amplifies the system instead.

In her video on egg dishes, she collected recipes and insights from home chefs around the world. From Cameroon to Albania to Singapore, each contributor is celebrated, and the viewer ends up informed, educated, and a bit more hopeful.

Beryl isn't the only star. She creates the stars.

This would have made no sense in the era of Julia Child when TV produced authoritative answers and untouchable stars. But in a connected system, where shares and comments are the engines of awareness, it flows.

49. ESTHER CHANGED THE WORLD

In 1983, Esther Dyson began editing a small newsletter: the real kind, on blue paper, sent with a stamp, to paying subscribers. By 1987, it came out every month, and cost $700 a year to subscribe. Subscribers to RELease 1.0 were also invited to an annual conference she hosted.

At its peak, the newsletter had fewer than 5,000 subscribers. But the demographics and attitude of her audience more than made up for its size. Every venture capitalist, investor, and tech media company was paying attention to the newsletter—partly because everyone else was paying attention.

Esther offered two things: She had the guts to go first and make assertions about what was next in tech. And second, she was the coordinator. By curating the topics to be discussed and laying out a point of view, she gave the tech industry an agenda.

The more she did it, the more valuable it became. She changed the system and then became part of the system.

She made millions of dollars from the newsletter and far more from her investments. But even more important is the fact that she made an impact.

50. SHINE A LIGHT

The Innocence Project has already freed 250 victims of unjust prosecution. That number should be 100 times greater, but it's also an astonishing act of generosity, insight, and dedication.

The system that sends innocent people to prison isn't often subject to close public inspection. Most of the people working in the system, regardless of their best intentions, face time and budget pressures as well as political pushback. It's simply easier to process one more case and send one more person to jail than it is to do the sort of investigation we expect from watching too much TV.

What the Innocence Project has done is turn the systemic bias toward ease on its head. It's easier to address a case that the Innocence Project has taken on than it is to try to fight them or ignore them. Small successes lead to bigger ones.

The ultimate goal is to have enough impact so that each conviction becomes a big deal to the system and not business as usual.

51. BIG PROBLEMS DEMAND SMALL SOLUTIONS

Big problems get big because systems amplify problems and make them sticky.

It's tempting to decide that a chronic problem is big enough that we ought to declare war on it, drop everything, hyperinvest, hold our breath, and do nothing until it is solved. But that's not how the problem got here and it might not be the best way for the problem to be solved.

We have the agency to decide and the chance to choose our path forward. But it's a path—a stepwise approach to a long-term impact. Too often we focus on power, the sudden windfall, and the big win. But what might be needed is community action to adjust the rewards and information flows involved in the system we're part of.

These small changes get deep into the workings of how the nodes in the system make decisions. System changes are more permanent and resilient than the more satisfying broad strokes we often embrace.

Important solutions aren't the work of right now. They are the persistent yet impatient work of building a strategy that's effective.

Every one of the elegant strategies mentioned above taps into the systems that exist. Each also makes a change happen and begins to construct systems that the creators want to build.

52. "GETTING THE WORD OUT" (ALSO KNOWN AS "SELFISH SHOUTING")

This is the mantra of the self-absorbed, short-term, hype-hustling promoter calling themselves a marketer. They say a good idea needs endless promotion because people deserve to hear about it.

There's a better way to think about this: First, ten.

In two words, this is the secret of the new marketing.

Find ten people. Ten people who trust you/respect you/need you/ listen to you...

Those ten people need what you have to sell or want it. And if they love it, you win. If they love it, they'll each find ten more people (or a hundred, or a thousand, or perhaps as few as three). Repeat.

If they don't love it, you need a new product or more insight about the ten people you choose. Begin again.

When you serve the smallest viable audience, your idea spreads. Your business grows. Not as fast as you want, but faster than you could ever imagine.

This approach changes the posture and timing of everything you do.

We can no longer market to the anonymous masses. They're not anonymous and they're not masses. You can only market to people who are willing participants, like this group of ten.

The timing means that the idea of a stresful launch and press releases and the big unveiling is nuts. Instead, plan on the gradual build that turns into a tidal wave. Organize for it and spend money appropriately. The traditional curve of money spent (big hump, then tailing off) is precisely backward to what you actually need.

Effective marketing isn't about hype or hustle or even about getting the word out. Instead, it focuses on engaging with people who seek to engage with us. Our job is to find a resilient path forward by helping people get to where they hope to go.

53. USE, BE USED, OR CHANGE IT

The system is here. Our strategy exists to help us make a change happen. We can do that by seeing the system and then using it to push our work forward… or we can see the system and subvert it by exploiting its feedback loops to make it work differently.

It's almost impossible to allow ourselves to be used by the system and then, with nothing but hard work, change the system itself.

Countless small businesses played the game Google wanted them to. They learned about SEO, saw the algorithm, and went to work as unpaid hamsters on Google's wheel. If they did it just right, they got traffic, and perhaps they could turn that traffic into revenue.

Until Google changed the rules (again).

The system works because it fools us into believing that we're voluntarily making a decision—that our choices are actually our choices.

But this is often an illusion. The system (whichever system we're captured by) has limited our choices. We can "pick any card," but we rarely see the entire deck.

Yet we have a chance to see the system instead of merely being part of it.

Every strategy depends on being conscious of the change we seek to make and the systems that can amplify or impede our progress.

---

54. FREEDOM IS POSSIBLE

And yet many of us don't feel that way. Perhaps it's because the systems around us are optimized around obedience. Perhaps it's because freedom is frightening.

Freedom comes with responsibility. And so we deny our agency. We walk away from it instead of using it.

This freedom comes with choices. The alternatives are everywhere we look, and without a blueprint, the easiest thing to do is stay still. To embrace being stuck. To whine instead of lead.

In fact, we each have more power than we often admit.

55. GETTING CLEAR ABOUT THE BUSINESS MODEL

When we get compensated for creating value in a way that enables us to do it again, we've found a business model.

The pizza place turns flour and cheese into a slice and gets paid enough to cover the rent, salaries and make a profit.

The non-profit identifies donors who not only want to make a change happen but are willing to make contributions to enable the organization to do its work. Not everyone has the resources and a story of money that makes this possible, and the non-profit has to do the work to find, attract and keep these donors.

A jazz musician might break even from recordings, but those recordings enable her to get live gigs that not only pay the bills but feed her creative soul.

A useful business model has a few attributes:

- It gets easier over time. Past success makes future success more likely.

- It's a welcome contribution to the lives and projects of the people who are paying (in time or money) for the work.

- It's resilient. When the world changes, the model adjusts and persists or even thrives.

The tools of the internet have encouraged people to try to turn hobbies into jobs. We invest our heart and soul into a podcast or a movement, and hope that one day, it'll turn into a business. The journey to a business model is an investment, it doesn't work the first day. We find a strategy, and then spend time and money to go from an idea to a generative, persistent and scalable engine of growth.

While it doesn't work the first day, it needs to work eventually. Time is the unseen driver of strategy.

56. AND IT FLIES

Time flies like an arrow. If I break an egg and scramble it, it can't be unscrambled and put back in the shell. A student learns a new skill, an organization builds a community, a company builds an asset. We move forward relentlessly.

Fruit flies like a banana. If you want to attract the flies, it doesn't pay to order them to appear, or even to insist. Placing a ripe banana on the windowsill is enough to create the conditions for change to happen.

Time is fuel. Without time there's no point. Our experience of time determines our choices.

A few years ago, Lisa Nichols was sitting with her 87-year-old grandmother. "Lisa," her grandmother said, "when you're my age, your job is to sit in a rocking chair and tell people the stories and lessons of a life well lived."

Then she looked at Lisa and said, "and at your age, your job is to live a life worth talking about."

57. PASSION AND OUR BUSINESS MODEL

Pundits tell us to do what we're passionate about and the work will take care of itself.

This is a brittle strategy. Some people get paid for their hobbies, but not many.

The alternative is to decide to be passionate about what you do.

The business model is our job. It's the way we create value for others and get compensated for it—the work might be the change we seek to make, but our job is to be able to get paid to commit to it regularly. The business model is built on the traction of creating change. And change requires tension, scarcity and forward motion.

When we do our work as a professional, we show up to solve a problem for people who know they have a problem and who have the means to pay to solve it.

Some of our work is unpaid. It builds an asset. Our reputation, our experience, our network of trusted partners. Some of our work is directly related to our business model, and we charge a fair price for it. And often, we simply create value without regard for whether it matches our model.

A healthy career and a useful project will have countless moments where we're not getting paid. Optimizing for the business model isn't the point. Creating a project with a solid business model, though, gives us the freedom to find even more passion in our work.

58. THE CIRCLE OF US AND THE CIRCLE OF NOW

A toddler wants what they want. Right now. Or a tantrum ensues.

As we mature, we expand our circles. Instead of focusing on just ourselves, we consider our family or our neighbors. Over time, we realize that traditional boundaries of caste or class or geography are not real but imaginary, and so we productively include more and more people in our "we."

The expanding isn't merely a good feeling. It's also a practical and effective way to create culture and possibility.

Strategy helps us see that *now* is also easily extended. We can include yesterday and tomorrow in our experience of what's right in front of us. As we grow up, we learn that investing in tomorrow is smarter than always insisting that we get something today.

The Iroquois Confederacy lived by a simple principle: "In our every deliberation, we must consider the impact of our decisions on the next seven generations."

Strategy challenges us to make each circle bigger.

The circle of us can grow and include the people we interact with and the community we hope to lead.

And the circle of now embraces our relationship with time. Effort in the short run creates the conditions for the long run we'd like to live with.

Who do we want as leaders, neighbors, or co-workers? Selfish tantrums are for toddlers.

When we expand our circles, we are able to step into the possibility of better.

While the smallest circle of now is **this instant,** some people plan a week ahead while others imagine their life or the life of their kids.

The difficult part around long-term change is simple: that sort of effort is not *now* enough for most people.

59. SELLING SELFISH

This is easy. It's hardly selling to give individuals something that they want, right here, right now, without regard for the long-term or the impact on others.

So why haven't we devolved to all become selfish toddlers, burning down our future to get what we want in this moment? Why haven't we let fear and greed push us all the way into the swamp, unable to work together to produce anything of value? And why are we able to engage with others, create things of beauty, and invest in the future?

Because systems build a bridge between today and tomorrow. Systems enforce cultural norms that reward people who can expand their circle of us. Even though systems get stuck, they outperform the mythical cowboy, living alone with a horse and a bedroll.

Our strategy is to use systems, alter systems, and build systems that expand our circles in ways each of us couldn't do on our own.

60. NEXT GUEST, BEST GUEST

A simple way to see time is to think about launching a podcast.

Who would be the best guest you could imagine? Michelle Obama, Elvis Costello or Atul Gawande are the sort of home run interviews that podcasters dream of. But of course, none of these folks is eager to appear on your new podcast.

Who would be the guest just before them? Which person, if they had a good experience on your show, would make it really likely that your dream guest would say yes?

And so we work backwards, beginning with the end in mind. Which guest makes it likely we can welcome the guest who would open the door to our dream guest?

Unfurl it all the way backward, without skipping steps, until you've reached your brother-in-law or next door neighbor.

Most overnight successes, aren't.

5,000 years ago, cuneiform clay tablets contained algorithms—instructions on how to compute things like the size of a cistern.

Donald Knuth decoded one of these in 1972 and discovered that the algorithms often concluded with the phrase "this is the procedure."

The strategy is not a procedure. The strategy is not a to-do list or even a guarantee.

We're so hung up on getting an A and doing it right that we blindly follow whatever leader is purported to have access to the procedure. Our job in these instances is to fit in all the way, be off the hook, and follow the steps.

But that's not our *work*.

Our work is a method, but there isn't a checklist. The method is to see time and systems and to find a resilient path forward. In the words of Cleo, the mysterious math genius, "You are not locked into a single axiom system. You may invent your own, whenever you wish—just use your intuition and imagination."

Hope is not a plan.

61. SEEING STRATEGY CLEARLY

Strategy is a flexible plan that guides us as we seek to create a change. It helps us make decisions over time while working within a system.

Strategy is interesting because of the complexity of its two companions: time and systems. Time resets each day, bringing with it new chances to make new decisions. And systems involve the interconnections of multiple people (and their interests) over time.

A key aspect of strategic planning is understanding opportunity costs, which are the benefits foregone by choosing one option over another.

Strategy demands humility, because accurately predicting the future is impossible.

Strategy also involves anticipating and planning for the actions and reactions of other actors within the system. This means considering not only the direct effects of strategic choices but also the indirect effects that come from the responses of competitors, customers, and even the environment. The success of a strategy is contingent not only on your actions but also on the actions of others.

If you sell your time at the lowest possible price, you'll always be busy helping someone else get to where they're going.

Successful people figure out how to trade their time and their effort for the change they seek to make in the world.

62. A BLUEPRINT IS AN ASSERTION

The builder creates a two-dimensional representation of a three-dimensional building. Unrolling the plans, she says, "This is what we will build."

This is the plan for a house. It imagines what it will take to create and what it will be like to inhabit. It's a chance to live in a future that hasn't happened yet.

For each of us, our strategy lives in *four* dimensions. It's not simply a drawing of what we are hoping for. It includes time and interactions as well: step and response, call and repeat, trial and improvement.

Tomorrow is going to be here soon whether we plan for it or not. Showing up without a strategy is like building without a plan. It might work out, but it's unlikely.

We need to talk about our strategy. We need to write it down.

63. SHARING YOUR STRATEGY: THE MODERN BUSINESS PLAN

It's not clear to me why business plans are the way they are, but they're often misused to obfuscate, bore, and show an ability to comply with expectations. If I want the real truth about a business and where it's going, I'd divide the modern business plan into six sections:

1. Truth
2. Assertions
3. Alternatives
4. People
5. Money
6. Time

The truth section describes the world as it is. Footnote it if you want to, but tell us about the market you are entering, the needs that already exist, the competitors in your space, technology standards, the way others have succeeded and failed in the past. The more specific the better. The more ground knowledge the better. The more visceral the stories the better.

Do you see the system? The point of this section is to be sure that you're clear about the way you see the world and that you and I agree on your assumptions. This section isn't partisan. It takes no positions and simply states how things are.

If you're not talking about systems and the status quo in your truth section, it's incomplete.

Truth can take as long as you need to tell it. It can include spreadsheets, market share analysis, and anything I need to know about how the world works. We shouldn't disagree about anything in the truth section.

The assertions section is your chance to describe how you're going to change things. We will do X, and then Y will happen. We will build Z with this much money in this much time. We will present Q to the market and the market will respond by taking this action.

In this section, share your business model. The tension you're going to create. The scaffolding you will build.

This is the heart of the modern business plan. The only reason to launch a project is to change something, and I want to know what you're going to do and what impact it's going to have.

Of course, this section will be incorrect. You will make assertions that won't pan out. You'll miss budgets and deadlines and sales. So the alternatives section tells me what you'll do if that happens. How much flexibility does your product or team have? If your assertions don't pan out, is it over?

The people section rightly highlights the key element—who is on your team and who is going to join your team. *Who* doesn't mean their résumé. Instead, talk about their attitudes and abilities. Strip away the false proxies and labels and instead focus on skills, resilience and their track record in shipping.

The next section is all about money. Because projects = money + time. How much do you need, how will you spend it, what does cash flow look like, P&Ls, balance sheets, margins and exit strategies. What assets will you build?

Finally, for emphasis, time. What will be different a week or a month or a year after you launch? How will the unseen axis of time inform your planning, so you are leading and not following.

Your local venture capitalist might not like this format, but I'm betting it will help your team think through the hard issues more clearly.

64. INTUITION IS STRATEGY WITHOUT NARRATIVE

Successful hunches might have been enough in the past. But for the work that lies ahead, for the changes we seek to make, we need to talk about it.

Show your work.

Most of us show up to do our work—to do well enough on the test, to please the boss, to pay the bills, to feel connected….

But it's the discomfort of articulating and altering our strategy that pays the biggest dividends.

Working on the right things is the way forward. And writing them down is one way to confirm you're working on the right things.

65. THE THING ABOUT EFFORT

"Try harder."

They tell you to overcome your fear, develop better habits, take it personally, be vulnerable, and be sure to post it all online. The advice implies that if something wasn't wrong with your character, you'd have no trouble succeeding.

But going faster is useless if you're running in the wrong direction.

Strategy is a commitment to seeing the race course before we begin. Your effort is up to you.

Surfing is better when we see and understand the waves.

66. RESILIENCE AND LEVERAGE

The fastest way forward might not be the most reliable.

When the world stays as we expect, optimization is going to perform very well. We optimize by borrowing money, producing technology, and making bets for a very specific set of conditions.

A Formula 1 race car is very likely to win on the track, but will fail a hundred times if you try to run errands with it.

Leverage makes us brittle.

If you're in a competitive market, your strategy may require you to out-leverage your competitors. It doesn't do the Formula 1 driver any good to brag about how his slightly slower car can deal with potholes and traffic lights.

Too often, though, we celebrate the brittle head start without noticing that in the long run, the turtle did a lot better than anyone expected.

Steve Blank helped us see that if we want to understand the likelihood of a startup's success, we should ignore how much money they raised. What matters is customer traction.

Not everyone, someone.

If the customers stick around, that's good. If they bring their friends and colleagues, it's likely to be a success.

Inevitably, the project will change in response to those that use it. But without customer traction, nothing happens.

67. IT BARELY WORKS

This is the story of every new software innovation. In fact it's the story of almost everything engineers have ever created.

The first Wright Brothers plane flew a few hundred yards at a time.

The first version of VisiCalc was underpowered and had few functions.

The earliest bridges were shaky, unreliable, and made of vines.

This is true for when we learn to walk or to speak a new language— or even visit a new community.

The secret of successful product development isn't an innovation that bursts forth as a polished and finished product. Instead, it's sticking with something that is almost useless and nurturing, sharing, and improving it until we can't imagine living without it. The goal at the start is traction with a few, not perfection for the masses.

Not only for a product, but for the work of a baker early in their career, or of a coach working their way up the ranks.

And it's particularly true for system change over time. The first examples are always thinly populated and imperfect.

People who are finding traction rarely feel burned out. Burnout comes when our goals don't align with our strategy. We hope for something that doesn't arrive, waiting, apparently powerless, for the world to bring it to us.

Trying to be in two moments at once—today and the future we're wishing for—is exhausting. An effective strategy helps us bridge the two.

Strategies are the tailwind that transform a project that is barely there into one that is essential and useful.

68. THE MINIMUM VIABLE AUDIENCE

This has nothing to do with shipping junk. It's not an excuse for rushing, either.

Seeking customer traction means that time is part of your strategy. A little traction that leads to more traction.

Make something for the few. Something so extraordinary and powerful that they would miss it if it were gone. Something remarkable enough that they will tell the others.

Watch what they do and listen to what tomorrow's users want. Add that to your product.

Repeat.

Of course we begin with the minimum. That's a choice and an advantage, but it also puts us on the hook. If we fail with the small group, why do we think we've got a shot with the larger one?

69. AND THEN WHAT HAPPENS?

The blueprint goes first. It's an assertion not just about the end, but about the steps to get there. And then reality arrives.

"I will do this."
And then what happens?

"I will do that."
And then what happens?

We do something and the people (and the system they're in) respond. Then what happens?

This expands our circle of now.

70. TO KILL ALL THE WHALES

Organizing millions of humans in a conspiracy to kill as many whales as possible wasn't very difficult.

In 1846, the American whaling fleet reached its all-time peak, with 735 ships and approximately 70,000 people employed in the industry. The majority of these ships were hunting sperm whales, as their oil was considered the best quality for lighting.

Tens of thousands of men left their families and risked their lives to hunt whales.

Easy? Yes. All someone had to do was explain the value of whale oil. This led to industries that made lanterns, distributed oil, refined it, and brought the blubber to shore. It created demand for boats, sails, docks and sailors as well.

The sperm whale wasn't saved by a publicity campaign or people voluntarily cutting back on light. It was saved by the development of kerosene lanterns and then the discovery of oil in Pennsylvania.

The system didn't want to kill all the whales. All the system wanted was to make a profit by solving the problem of darkness. When it found a cheaper and more efficient way to do that, it did.

There are countless conspiracies. They're not a secret. We simply need to see the systems.

71. NOT ALL NEEDS HAVE A MARKET (YET)

A market is a category. A market is a place with competition. In a market, people have habits and budgets and social pressure to engage. And in a market, people make choices.

In many cultures, there's a market for all the items that go with a quinceañera—a traditional birthday party for a 15-year-old girl. While girls in other cultures might want the sort of attention that comes with this extravaganza, there might not be an market for it where they live.

It's tempting to be a market pioneer—to be the one who shows up with the first charge card, the first personal training firm, or the first home computer. But it's a challenging road.

It can be thrilling work, but because creators focus on needs and not markets, they often fail to account for how difficult it is to activate those needs and turn them into a thriving market if one doesn't exist yet.

If you're in market-creation mode, it helps to call it that and be prepared for how difficult it might be.

72. SEEING THE WINDMILL

If you've ever played miniature golf, you know that the best obstacle is the windmill. You need to get your ball past the windmill and into the hole while the blades slowly turn.

The strategy here is obvious and simple. Time it right and take your shot.

It gets a bit more complex when we're playing chess. Now there's another human involved. If you move your queen over there, your opponent will castle and put you in check, so you better not.

You do this, they do that.

But when we're playing rugby or ultimate frisbee, now we have to keep track of many humans on our team and theirs. What worked last play might not work this time.

Players in these free-flowing competitions don't repeat plays by rote. They flow, in sync, with a mixture of practiced movements and improvisation.

Most of the time, rugby is simple compared to our real life. There are hundreds of competitors, government agencies, new technologies, and other seemingly unrelated options, all entwined in a system over time.

Facing this, we often revert to playing putt-putt with a windmill. But we can do better than that. Windmills are predictably boring. The regular nature of the windmill is the point. The rest of the world is a lot more complex. Recognizing this is the purpose of the expanding circle of us.

73. WITHOUT A STRATEGY

The meme says, "We do this not because it is easy...but because we thought it would be easy."

Too often, strategic conversations are used to amplify resistance and to push us to take no action. The blueprint is too complicated, the odds are too long, and there are too many steps. It's better to stay home.

And this history can lead to the well-meaning but misguided step of simply beginning. Beginning with optimism and verve but no strategy.

While the urge to begin may increase your chances of starting, it also pushes you toward failure—failure that's particularly difficult because the costs are higher.

If you care about the work to be done, it's worth verbalizing and testing your strategy.

At each step from when you begin until the change is achieved, there's a system at work. Some people can voluntarily say yes or no. There are community and cultural expectations, status roles and affiliation at stake. And there are network effects and feedback loops that either slow you down or push you forward.

The blueprint is a firm foundation for forward motion. It sustains us when we hit a momentary roadblock and keeps us on track when it seems as though there are too many interesting choices.

74. SOME REASONS WE AVOID HAVING A STRATEGY

- We're not able to see the system

- We see the system but we can't choose between working with it or on it

- We'd prefer to get the benefits of our actions sooner rather than later

- It's often more satisfying to be picked by a powerful system than to alter it

- We're concerned that our strategy won't work and we don't want to fail

- We're concerned that our strategy will work and we hesitate to embrace the responsibility that would come with that

- We've been indoctrinated to follow instructions and ask for tactics

- It's easier to go along with the crowd than to persuade them of a more effective but arduous path

- Sunk costs are difficult to ignore

- Projects are intimidating to manage

It's tempting to daydream about the future, but we're not sure we're ready to live there.

75. A FRAMEWORK FOR A STRATEGY

- **Awareness** of the system and the rules. Any change we seek to make involves scarcity, the status quo, networks, and what came before. Most of all, it involves awareness of time and the distance from today until tomorrow.

- **Empathy** for the individuals who must engage with your project. We don't need to have sympathy or agreement to realize that other people have the independence and power to make choices, and those choices will always be based on their experience, worldview, and self-interest.

- **Choices** are available to each of us. We have more agency than we'd like to admit, and our decisions can be better aligned with the goals of the project.

- **Uncertainty** is a feature of every strategy. Not the delineated steps of a proven process, but the exploration and probabilities of creating a better version of the future.

- **Resilience** comes from acknowledging that the x-axis is time, and that today is not the same as tomorrow. Few projects work as we intend, and our strategy embraces the truth that our plans will change.

- **Resources** involve a clear understanding of what's available to execute the strategy. This includes financial resources, human capital, technology, and other assets that can be leveraged to achieve the desired outcomes.

76. CREATING THE CONDITIONS FOR CHANGE

People don't do things because you want them to. They change because *they* want to.

The same is true for complex systems.

Our job is to create the conditions for the ones we work with to make a choice that aligns with the change we seek to make. Strategic work isn't a form of stalling, and it doesn't minimize the emergency of right now. Instead, it embraces the fact that we succeed when we commit to culture change instead of first aid.

Culture defeats tactics every time, which is why strategy is often about creating culture.

"What's it like around here?" is a question that rarely gets discussed, but it's never unconsidered. If we can create the system dynamics for forward motion, the rest of our work gets much easier.

Once we create the culture and tap into the systems, change happens organically. Heroic self-control, persistent effort, and the desire to do it all ourselves are a recipe for frustration.

Skiing works better if there's snow and you're headed downhill. Too often, we blame our lack of effort or skill when the real problem is that we went to the wrong hill. It's still our mistake, but a different sort of error.

We can intentionally be in the right place at about the right time. We can actively find high-leverage moments to shift our odds. And we can relentlessly make better decisions that match the change we seek to make.

I grew up in Buffalo, NY, and learned about driving in snow. The first truth is that stopping the car is harder than you think, and that means that snow tires are the single best way to stay safe. The second truth is that a car in motion is much easier to drive than one that is already stuck.

Both insights involve traction. The first recognizes the traction needed to make forward motion so you can get to where you're going. And the other recognizes that traction is always easier when your strategy is aligned with the world you live in.

Our strategy sets us up for success when it's based in the reality of the systems all around us, the desires of those we need to work with, and the insight to embrace resilience instead of insisting that the world align with our needs at all times.

77. TWELVE SLOGANS

What do we talk about when we talk about strategy? Consider these building blocks:

- The future is an unvisited city, but we can see it from a distance

- The audience can be chosen

- Don't play games you can't win

- Projects can be managed

- We make decisions

- A difference can be made

- Assets can be built

- Networks can be created

- Traction is the way forward

- Sunk costs can be ignored

- Organizations change

- You're not sitting in traffic—you are traffic

78. UNSEEN SYSTEMS AND UNINTENDED CONSEQUENCES

Unseen systems conceal and undermine our agency. They fool us into believing we have fewer choices than we do.

We're all participants in the systems around us and complicit in their consequences even if we didn't intend them. We first need to see the systems and then we have the opportunity to work to change them.

We make a difference by seeing the system and dancing with it. We can work with a system to achieve our goals, and we can change a system over time.

The first step is seeing the system, and the second step is to commit to a strategy for change.

Our blueprint begins with three questions:

- Who is it for?

- What is it for?

- What is the system?

We can't change everyone, and we can't change everything, but if we're specific, generous, and persistent, we might be able to change enough.

All human interactions live in systems, and we can either work within the system or work to change it.

Tasks fill our days, but strategies determine whether we've wasted our effort.

Effort is often part of our work, but effort by itself is not a strategy.

79. WE ARE NOT PLANKTON

In Russian, they call them Офисный планктон—office plankton. Low-level workers who simply follow instructions. It's a perfect image, and more widespread than ever. Many CEOs are office plankton as well, floating along and simply following the crowd.

It's tempting to decide that if we can't be fully in charge, the best option is simply to be office plankton. It lets us off the hook.

But in truth we have more freedom, agency, and influence than we dare to imagine. Yet acting on these doesn't involve climbing a pyramid or achieving a position of ultimate authority.

While there are hierarchies all around us, it's more useful to realize that we are all part of a web. A network of interconnections, a system of systems, where influence and affiliation are more useful than dominance or power.

It's easier to create media hype about a powerful cabal that controls us, but the most compelling strategies come from systems and the culture, not from someone in charge.

Resilient and long-lasting change travels horizontally, not vertically. It's cultural, based in systems and communications, not dictated.

80. STRATEGIC MARKETING

Marketing is the art of building a product or service that tells a story. A true story—one that resonates and changes the person who experiences it.

The first job of the marketer is to find a problem and to solve it, helping the customer get to where they are going.

And the second, which (from a marketing perspective) is ultimately more important than the first, is to give that person a story to tell others. To engage with the web of community. To help that person improve their status and affiliation because they are engaging with others using the story that you helped them create.

When we see the world as a web, and our work as helping the people in the web connect and grow, the strategy becomes far more clear.

81. NO TIME TO WASTE

Of course there isn't.

Time is all we've got.

Time is all there is.

Time is not only the calendar or the clock. Time is the scarce resource that fuels every project and bounds every strategy.

We can't waste time because it's not ours to waste. It's simply the way we keep track of everything else.

82. STRATEGY AND AIMLESSNESS

Can we find joy without a strategy? Do we need to optimize every interaction or schedule every moment? Do we need an appointment to smell the flowers or a watch to track our exertion when we're out for a walk?

There are systems that would like to suck us into a fully quantified life, one where satisfaction is a combination of measured productivity and how many followers we have. I hope that all of us realize that this is a dead end and not the point.

The focus of strategic thinking begins with "What's it for?" While some of our days are spent in pursuit of a specific change, of an outcome, of an impact we hope to make, our life doesn't have to be.

The successful blueprint aligns the change you seek to make with the life you seek to live.

83. SHOULD MIGHT BE A TRAP

- Do the things you need to do to get what you need in the long run.

- Don't do the things that keep you from creating the change you seek.

"Should" is the insistence of culture to cause us to conform to the systems it cares about—but should might not be what you need to make a difference.

84. WHERE IS THE BLUEPRINT?

"Whenever a building is constructed, you usually have an architect who draws a blueprint, and that blueprint serves as the pattern, as the guide, and a building is not well erected without a good, solid blueprint.

Now each of you is in the process of building the structure of your lives, and the question is whether you have a proper, a solid and a sound blueprint.

I want to suggest some of the things that should begin your life's blueprint. Number one in your life's blueprint, should be a deep belief in your own dignity, your own worth and your own somebodiness. Don't allow anybody to make you feel that you are nobody. Always feel that you count. Always feel that you have worth, and always feel that your life has ultimate significance...

Secondly, in your life's blueprint you must have as a basic principle the determination to achieve excellence in your various fields of endeavor. You're going to be deciding as the days and the years unfold what you will do in life—what your life's work will be. And once you discover what it will be, set out to do it well.

And I say to you, my young friends, doors are opening to each of you—doors of opportunities that were not open to your mothers and your fathers—and the great challenge facing you is to be ready to enter these doors as they open."

The Rev. M.L. King Jr., to a group of students in 1967

85. SOONER OR LATER

There are no charging stations anywhere near Smoke Lake in Algonquin Park, Canada. That means that you'll need to charge your car before you get there, or you'll end up stranded.

We understand this intuitively. "Last fill-up for 400 miles" means you need to stop even if you're not about to run out of gas—because, in fact, you *will* run out of gas.

Strategy always involves a delay. We need to do something non-obvious or un-fun now so we can get the result we seek later.

And that requires trust. Trust in our understanding of what's being offered, and trust that the world won't let us down.

That's why disadvantaged individuals (either by personal experience or unearned low social standing) are often trapped in a downward spiral. Strategy requires an investment in the future, one we need resources and confidence to make. And making that investment in the future can increase our confidence and resources in return.

The marshmallow test posits that it can predict a toddler's future from a simple test. The three-year-old is given a marshmallow. "I'm going to leave the room for ten minutes. If you can wait until I get back, I'll give you a bonus marshmallow. But if you eat it while I'm gone, that's all you get." Apparently, grit and self-control at this age indicate good things for the future.

But a child is unlikely to hold out for two marshmallows if they are growing up in a home with not enough food, or if they're familiar with broken promises and stress. For many, "take what you can get" is a reasonable survival strategy.

We're all living in a marshmallow test, every day. Seeing where the delays exist can give us the confidence to invest today to make an impact tomorrow.

"Don't eat the marshmallow" is a lot easier to work with if you understand and trust the path to getting that bonus marshmallow.

86. STRATEGY IS THE PARTNER OF FREEDOM

- The freedom to create, to write, to invent, and to share widely.

- The freedom to connect, to reach out to nearly every everyone.

- The freedom to learn and to teach.

- The freedom to choose the information we consume, the time we spend, and the people we associate with.

It's true that the world is still filled with barriers, limits, and injustice. And it's also the case that we never have enough time or enough resources to do all that we might want to do.

And yet we waste the freedom we each have. We waste it waiting for instructions, and we waste it meandering without a strategy.

We each have the freedom to care, to connect, to choose, to initiate, and to do work that matters.

If we choose.

When the person you could have been meets the person you are becoming, is it going to be a cause for celebration or heartbreak?

This is something we must work on right now, and tomorrow, and every single day until the meeting happens.

87. THE LOTTERY IS NOT A STRATEGY

Someone is going to win the Megamillions lottery.

But it's not going to be you and it won't be me.

Too often, our approach to our work is to view it as a repeated chance to buy a very low-odds lottery ticket.

This approach is always outperformed in the long run by consistent and persistent strategic work.

Strategic work is a blueprint for where we're headed. It's far more than a goal. It's a deliberate statement about the world as we see it, the systems as we understand them, and the probabilities of our assertions working out. Our blueprint describes how effort now will turn into impact later, and it is built around empathy and traction.

This puts us on the hook because we can challenge ourselves (and be challenged by our peers) about the quality of our reasoning, and we can improve it along the way.

The lottery, on the other hand, is ultimately a shiny and seductive dead end, because even if we win now and then, we have no agency and don't learn as we go.

88. NOSTALGIA FOR THE FUTURE

A strategy is the most reliable way to get to a future we'd like to live in.

Originally, "nostalgia" referred to homesickness. A desire to get back to a place we miss. However, that desire can be addressed simply by getting on a bus.

It evolved to the nostalgia we're familiar with today. A nostalgia for a past—one that's predictable, safe, and completely unattainable, because time machines don't go in that direction.

We can choose to enjoy nostalgia (the popular kind, nostalgia for the past). We gladly suffer from that bittersweet feeling we get about events that we loved but can't relive. The unattainability of the past is part of its attractiveness.

We'd love to do it again, but we can't.

Nostalgia for the future is that very same feeling about things that haven't happened yet. We are prepared for them to happen, but if something comes along to change our future, those things won't happen, and we'll be disappointed.

We're good at visualizing this future, though if we think it's not going to happen, we get nostalgic for it, giving up before we've had a chance to make it real.

This isn't positive visualization. It's attachment of the worst sort. We're attached to an outcome, often one we can't control.

Instead of attachment and a relentless addiction to one and only one outcome, we can develop a resilient strategy that helps us build the future we seek to live in.

We can choose to get on the bus. To go build that future we're yearning for.

89. DOING OUR JOB OR DOING OUR WORK?

When we're doing our job, there's a checklist. Instructions. Deniability. Sooner or later we have to do our jobs, but it probably pays to focus on our work.

Our work makes change happen. Our work is up to us. Our work is a series of choices that lead to the jobs we spend our hours on.

Our work is our responsibility and our opportunity.

Our job requires answering questions. Our work gives us a chance to ask them.

Where did your job come from? It came from the system you're in. The system trained you to do the tasks. The system might be a social media network or it might be an educational institution. You might be a barber or a landlord. The system gives us our job.

The work is to figure out which job we actually want.

90. TENSION FIRST AND ABOVE ALL

We talk about tension as if it's a bad thing. But the only way to launch a rubber band across the room is to pull it backwards, creating tension. Tension permits the water spider to walk across a puddle without drowning. And tension keeps us focused on the world around us.

When we arrive with the change we seek to make, we are causing tension. There's always tension associated with change—the people we serve wonder, "Will it work, can I ignore it, what are other people doing, will this make me look stupid, am I qualified, will I be left out, what is everyone else doing, what will it cost me, can I leave the other choices behind?"

The strategy we adopt has tension at its center. We're not here to "do our job." We're here to make a change happen.

A good idea isn't based on what you would do if you could start over. A good idea is a series of leverage points and disruptions that would permit a change agent to create tension and opportunity that might bend a system in the right direction.

When our work interacts with a system, tension is created or we're ignored.

When Google launched Gmail, there were a limited number of trial accounts. Getting an account satisfied the curiosity of early adopters and gave them status. They didn't want to be left out, and so they scrambled, trading attention for the chance to go first.

Once they were in the beta test, these users discovered that the utility was worth the hassle of switching email providers.

Of course, one of the visible side effects of using email is that your email is seen by others. They didn't have to sign up or give permission to receive these gmail.com notes from others—that's how email works. Using it spreads the word.

Early in the launch, "normal" people were getting emails from influential tech leaders in their circles, each with this new gmail.com address.

This change caused new circles of tension. Should I switch to this new thing? And the change caused conversations. People were talking about the new service without Google asking them to.

The network grew. Gmail reached a million users in two weeks, and now has 1.5 billion users.

But the same sort of tension exists at a very minor scale. The tension of changing the culture in a first-grade classroom. The tension of opening a new shop in town.

91. THE FASTEST CYCLIST IN THE WORLD

In 1933, Francis Faure smashed the record for the farthest distance traveled in one hour on a bicycle. It had stood for twenty years, but Faure beat it easily.

He had a better bike.

Unfortunately for Charles Mochet, the bike's creator, Francis Faure wasn't a world-class bike racer. He was clearly in the second or third rank of wannabe racers.

When Faure showed up with his recumbent bike (in which the rider leans backward and the pedals are far forward), the high-status riders jeered at him. "Faure, you must be tired and want to go to take a nap on that thing. Why don't you sit up upright and pedal like a man?"

They had a status quo to defend. Not only their equipment, but their standing and technique were all tied up in the more traditional style of bike.

The story of the new bike was clear. It offered a technical hack that would help lesser riders increase their status, and so it threatened the hierarchy. In addition, it undermined the sunk costs of skill and equipment that the dominant riders had amassed. Finally, it challenged the dominance of the existing bike manufacturers, who were also the sponsors of the races.

Immediately after his triumph, the governing body of bike racing met and after much debate, banned recumbent bikes from competition—a ban that remains nearly a hundred years later. As a result, manufacturers continue to focus on building the bikes pros want to ride, and amateurs follow the lead of the pros, controlling distribution and lowering prices, and so the system persists.

People like us do things like this.

Even if you aren't going to win, you'd like to look like you could.

In 2024, *Bicycling* magazine wrote an article about how much pain traditional bikes can cause, particularly for women. It chronicled that some riders are even having labial surgery so they won't have to give up their bikes.

People are having significant surgery instead of simply switching to a recumbent bike.

A recumbent bike is faster, safer, and more comfortable. Even though most riders are unlikely to ever win a competition, the system has enough influence on their status and how they affiliate with others that they'd rather have painful, expensive surgery than switch to a "better" bicycle.

Better might not mean faster and more comfortable. It might simply be the kind the others want.

If Mochet had hired a world-champion cyclist to be his influencer, the entire story would have been transformed. Jealousy and the status quo are powerful forces.

92. WHEN DID APPLE BECOME APPLE?

The world's most valuable company had its roots in a garage, where Steve Wozniak created the first widely available and well-priced home computer.

But there was no system then. Only a few computer stores and almost no one writing programs for home computer owners. There was no one buying ads, so no magazines in which they could run.

The Apple II planted the seeds for the system that would follow. But if all Apple had done was make more versions of the Apple home computer, it would have been the end of their story.

So the world's most valuable company ended up borrowing/stealing/finding the technological insights that led to the Macintosh. They bet a big chunk of the company that the Mac would take off and change the world.

The operating system had an appealing design. The box was charming. The Super Bowl ad created a legend.

But none of it would have mattered without the work of Guy Kawasaki.

Guy invented the job of computer evangelist. He spent more than a year traveling around the US, persuading programmers to develop software for the Mac.

He danced with Aldus and Adobe and Microsoft and Spinnaker and a thousand other companies.

He built a new ecosystem, creating a foundation so that users would demand software which would lead companies to make it, which would reward them to run ads and support stores that carried their products.

And then what happens?

The iPhone is here because there was an ecosystem and a strategy to take it forward.

93. WHEN DID NETFLIX BECOME NETFLIX?

Netflix began as a DVD rental company. Ubiquitous red envelopes and a huge selection were the hallmarks of their early success.

After they defeated Blockbuster and had the market to themselves, Reed Hastings and Ted Sarandos made a strategic decision to shift the future of the company to streaming movies and original programming. And they communicated this commitment in a very simple way:

They stopped inviting the DVD leadership team to meetings.

Even though DVD rentals were all of their profit and most of their revenue, they knew that having these powerful voices in the room would ultimately lead to compromises designed to defend that line of business.

Our next move is often something that decreases the value of our previously hard-won assets.

94. WHEN DID DAVID BOWIE BECOME DAVID BOWIE?

If you listen to the original recordings of rock stars like Sly Stone, Janis Joplin and Lou Reed, you'll hear that they started out doing their best to sound exactly like everyone else.

That's what the system seems to reward. That's what gets you a producer and a demo and apparently, a shot at stardom. Except it almost never works.

The big step between musician and rock star is the decision to sound like yourself instead of seeking to sound like everyone else.

95. WHAT'S YOUR STRATEGY?

For our parents, a strategy was reserved for MBAs at big companies or the diplomats who ran countries. Alcoa and Kodak had a strategy; so did Winston Churchill. Maybe Muhammad Ali had a strategy for his next fight, but for the typical human, that wasn't part of our job.

The TV networks came up with a strategy for what they would make and what we would watch. We consumed what we were offered.

Now, though, in the midst of the great fracturing, the strategy is largely up to us. From the innocuous choices about what media to consume (or to create) all the way up to the existential strategies of what sort of world we want to build and live in.

This might be the right moment to understand our power and to do something with it.

Tomorrow keeps arriving. Perhaps we can choose a strategy to make it better.

96. WHAT DOES IT MEAN TO BE A STRATEGIC THINKER?

It means that you see the system.

It means that you develop the assets and skills that you will need to work with the system or to change it.

It means that you have the empathy to understand how others make choices.

And it means that you work to reduce delays in the feedback loops so you can adjust your tactics based on the system's response to your work .

The operating plan and tactics that accompany our strategy are focused on these feedback loops—on allowing us to become more nimble when we encounter responses from the status quo.

97. TACTICS ARE NOT STRATEGIES

Tactics are how we win short-term games. Tactics are flexible, disposable, and sometimes secret.

Strategies are for the long-term games. Strategies are worth sharing, inspecting, and sticking with.

A tactic is what we do next. A strategy is all the nexts, one after the other.

Tactics are for now. Strategies see and respect and value time.

If your tactics work, they should advance your strategy.

If your strategy is flawed, all the successful tactics you engage in won't help.

98. WHAT'S A FEEDBACK LOOP?

If the wedding DJ holds the microphone too close to the speakers, a horrible screech occurs. That's because the sound goes through the mic, gets amplified, and then goes out the speaker, and then back again, over and over.

Feedback loops work in the other way as well—someone robs a bank in the Old West, so they fortify the safe, and the next robber has a harder time, then they hire some guards, and on and on, and eventually, bank robberies start to fade away.

Feedback loops make rich people richer. They also power the system that leads each generation of computer to get faster, and for hospitals to invest more and more in technology.

Feedback loops aren't there to give you advice. Feedback loops either drive change forward or hold it back. They multiply or divide.

How did we end up with weddings that cost $2,000,000? A wedding is a semi-public ceremony. It celebrates connection and status. Many people who attend a wedding will either host a wedding for their kids or plan one for themselves. When they do, they take the standards of the weddings they've attended and are likely to ratchet them forward. The feedback loop is amplified.

A politician gets attention by doing something outrageous. The next politician seeking attention works to outdo the first one. Quickly, the standards for decorum are replaced by an attention-seeking feedback loop that races to the bottom. And the news media follows along, amplifying and being amplified by the loop.

A fancy hotel has plenty of well-paying guests. An external event (a shift in culture, a regional downturn, a pandemic) causes occupancy to drop off. The hotel responds by investing a bit less in food and upkeep. So fewer people return. And the loop continues, until the hotel is no more.

If you see a feedback loop, you're seeing a system at work.

99. TIME ISN'T FREE

Every choice comes with a cost. When we spend an hour reading a book, it's an hour we didn't spend listening to speed metal. When we take on one client, we've chosen not to pursue a different option.

Opportunity cost is real, and as we've been given more access, more tools, and more opportunities, the cost continues to increase.

Strategies recognize that our time comes at a cost, and challenge us to choose.

You're spending your time whether you realize it or not. And without a strategy, the time you spent is wasted.

When we recognize that time today is the investment we make to transform our lives tomorrow, the invisible axis becomes even more obvious.

The choices we make today to make tomorrow better are our strategy.

100. AVOIDING HINDSIGHT BIAS

Most business theories fall into an easy trap: They find a few successful examples and then explain how their theory explains their success.

Of course, they aren't clear how their theory doesn't apply to all the similar businesses that failed.

The reliance on hindsight bias often leads individuals to mistakenly believe they possessed advance knowledge of an event's outcome, falsely convincing themselves that they could predict the event without empirical evidence, merely through logical deduction.

In truth we still don't know. We don't know why Facebook succeeded and Friendster failed. Why General Magic struggled but Airbnb made it to the other side.

Anyone who promises a detailed road map is unaware of how complex creating the future is.

All we can do is look for the right conditions, not expect a guarantee.

101. NOT THE PARTS, THE SYSTEM

When more than one person (or in the case of things like cars, one part) is working with others to create something in coordination, it's a system.

Improving the parts of the system doesn't always improve the output of the system, because, as Russ Ackoff has written, the system is about the interconnections between the parts, not the parts themselves. Put an efficient bicycle tire on a truck and the truck won't work better. And yet we spend our time fixing tires, not looking at trucks.

If you seek to be part of a system, it helps to understand how your actions will change the system, and it helps even more if you can discover how the system will respond or react to your actions.

102. THINKING ABOUT "STATUS"

It's mentioned more than fifty times in this book, and it's a critical component of systems and strategy. But we often confuse it with an easily measured metric that is sometimes (but not always) a measure of status: money.

In some circles, rich people have status. Buying an expensive car is a way of hinting that you are rich, and that might give you status.

But the class clown in third grade had a sort of status. So did the head of the glee club.

Status is "who eats lunch first" (at least at this watering hole).

There's status awarded to the tall kid, and to the one that gets good grades. In some circles there's status for someone who has a lot of online social media followers.

And then there's status for people who appear to shun easily measured proxies of status.

103. SEEING STATUS IN HOLLYWOOD

Among the top 500 grossing Hollywood movies of all time, *My Big Fat Greek Wedding* is the most profitable in return on investment.

And among all Hollywood movies in the top 1,500 at the box office, *Paranormal Activity* is far and away the highest return, outperforming almost any investment the stock market has ever offered. The return on investment was over a million percent.

One wonders why movies like these aren't made very often, rarely win awards, or get adoring previews in the hype media.

The answer lies in affiliation and status. The directors, stars, and producers who work in Hollywood don't devote themselves to this craft to earn the maximum return for their investors.

They do it to participate in a system that produces affiliation and status.

Most industries have similar objectives. They're not as easy to notice, though.

Who's up and who's down?

What the system makes is probably what the system values. And vice versa.

104. THE OUTPUT OF SYSTEMS

Systems produce what they produce, not what the organizers or participants might have been hoping for.

The healthcare system doesn't make health. It makes treatments. Sometimes health is a by-product.

The higher education system in the US doesn't work to produce well-informed graduates. It makes careers and culture.

The typical corporation doesn't transform its customers. It enriches its executives. The transformation is an occasional side effect.

It's uncommon for surprising system outputs to be a deliberate conspiracy. Because systems are not simply unrelated nodes, the outputs and combinations can end up disappointing us. As people work together, the side effects cease to be trivial and often become the entire point of the enterprise.

105. OUR INTENT IS ALTERED BY THE SYSTEM WE'RE PART OF

The Dartmouth Atlas study of health care has shown that when the number of hospital beds available increases, the number of patients admitted to the hospital increases. The same is true for medical devices and tests.

It's not only teachers who "teach to the test." We all do.

Like gravity, the systemic forces on us are invisible and feel normal. Culture is the enforcement dynamic of resilient systems, and culture is the way things are around here.

The invisible (and sometimes visible) pressures of systemic gravity offer us status and affiliation if we'll stick with the culture.

As long as culture is delivering the resilient and useful results we seek, there's no issue at all. But when it's no longer fulfilling, it might be worth looking hard at the system we've decided to support and the systems we're building.

106. THE BIRTH OF AFYA

In 2007, Danielle Butin was traveling in Tanzania. A trained occupational therapist, she had been working as a healthcare executive in the burgeoning industry of elder care.

On the trip, she met a doctor from London who was donating her time at a local clinic. The woman was distraught. "At home, I can make a difference. I have the supplies and tools I need to offer healthcare to my ill patients. Here, I'm useless. Even the simplest bandages and antiseptics aren't available. I'm watching patients die and I'm powerless to help."

This planted the seed for a strategy that has transformed the lives of hundreds of thousands of people.

Butin discovered that hospitals in the US are required by law to discard drugs and supplies long before their useful life is over. Sealed, sterile, and potent lifesaving items are thrown out by the ton. The drug companies don't mind (it increases sales), the FDA wants to maximize efficacy and sterility, and the cost of resorting each item would be very high, so hospitals comply.

Afya is a bridge between multiple systems. They take unused or expired medical devices and supplies from the United States and bring them to healthcare systems in countries that can put them to good use.

Beginning with a trip to a temporary storage room in the basement of one hospital where items went before being thrown out, Afya has grown to become a worldwide force.

It's instructive to see how each element in the system eagerly participates, because it illustrates the power of a strategy to take good intentions and turn them into action.

Hospital administrators are often horrified at the level of waste that their systems create. They are open to shifting the waste stream away from a landfill to a more productive use overseas.

Doctors are too busy to spend weeks in Haiti or Ukraine, but know that their influence at the local hospital can make a difference in healthcare, which is precisely what they signed up for when they began their careers.

Donors are often motivated to pay for something as tangible and urgent as a container ship bringing tons of essential medical aid to Puerto Rico or Tanzania, where it's desperately needed and a simple transaction can unlock enormous benefits.

Local health groups on the ground are eager to have useful supplies, and when they understand that their autonomy is protected, can put their skills and network to use.

There are countless good causes. But Butin's strategy involved seeing how different systems could engage with each other to produce an outcome that each participant is proud to be part of.

107. PERPETUATING THE SCAM

A system rarely serves everyone involved, and yet they're difficult to change. For example: People entering the workforce aren't served well by the existing system, and neither are the organizations that seek to hire them.

The system for finding a job is unfair, inefficient and opaque. And once hired, new employees are often poorly trained, waste time in meetings and struggle to find a way to contribute.

And yet, once employees move up a rung or two, once they become management, they participate on the other side—relying on the very same system.

Medical students find their training to be exhausting and dehumanizing, but the ones who stick it out to become doctors don't do much to change the system they just participated in.

This isn't because they're not good humans. It's because persistent systems are good at sticking around. For any given individual, it seems like there's nothing to be done about it. We often get precisely what the system promises us we'll get, and sometimes we get stuck and accept this, regardless of the consequences.

Creating tomorrow by repeating yesterday is not a useful way forward.

108. TOXIC SYSTEMS

Systems don't start out to be selfish, but resilient ones often end up that way.

The beauty and fashion industry doesn't serve all of its customers. Some end up struggling with issues of self-esteem and health. Others find themselves victims of misogyny that undermines their ability to contribute. And the ecological devastation caused by discarding tons of fast fashion costs all of us.

The internet began with laudable goals of connection, knowledge, and fun. But social networks, dark patterns, and surveillance capitalism have caused many to lose hope, while dividing us and creating despair.

When a system creates negative effects, it almost always happens gradually. Each node makes what feels like a reasonable decision at every step along the way, until the descent is far greater than we signed up for.

There's cultural pressure and momentum to go along, and before long we're trapped—unable to get off social media, in debt, feeling stuck.

Toxic systems don't go away on their own. Community action and peer support give us the scaffolding we need to build new systems. As those gain traction and power, the original system begins to take notice and alter its behavior.

109. THE URGENCY OF "NO"

If scarcity is one of the elements of a game, we benefit from embracing the fact that we can't have everything, do everything, or offer everything.

Every strategy requires choices. And those choices often involve saying "no" to things we *could* do, but *won't* do.

- We will turn away customers.

- We will avoid some opportunities.

- We will focus on one thing at the expense of another.

It's tempting to fill our days with work. To update our TikTok, LinkedIn, and Facebook pages, then shift to Instagram and then back to our email. To work through an endless list of tasks and check off all the boxes. And to serve every customer, every constituent, and every colleague, even when we might be more generous to simply send them somewhere else.

If we're competing with everyone, in every venue, it's no wonder we're not getting much done.

110. ON BEING JUDGED

How do you decide who has the power to judge you?

If you're competing in the Olympic figure skating finals, it's pretty clear who the judges are. They sit in a special box and hold signs.

When competing for a gold medal, it's not helpful to ignore the judges or even to act as though you didn't sign up to be judged by them, because you did.

Most of the time, though, the identity of the judges isn't nearly as clear. There are potential judges everywhere we look. It's tempting to imagine that everyone is a judge, or to boldly assume that no one is.

A foundation of our blueprint is acknowledging which judges we are prepared to choose, and which wannabe judges we're eager to ignore.

111. CHOOSE YOUR CUSTOMERS AND CHOOSE YOUR FUTURE

Every project has customers. It might be the patients your non-profit serves, or your donors. It might be the person who walks into the coffee shop to deal with you when you're working as a clerk, or it might be your boss.

As the song says, "You've got to serve somebody."

When we choose our customers, we embrace their worldview and the system they are part of. Their budgets become our budgets. Their priorities become ours as well.

Customers can be a choice. We can be passive and take what we get, or we can choose to be active and seek out the customers we'd like to work with.

It used to be simple. The customer walked into your shop and gave you money. There was a retail storefront, a way of getting the word out, and the customer.

You no longer have to take all orders or simply wait for who's next. Instead, we have a chance to send a message and let potential customers know who we're there for.

Here are some of the choices that customers and clients dictate:

- The price

- Support and service

- Exclusivity

- Co-creation

- Durability

- The status it brings

- Public persona of the brand

- Sustainability

If you set out to serve very demanding clients that expect custom work, low prices, and plenty of personal service, that is how you'll spend your days.

If you raise your prices 30%, you might exchange your value-seeking customers for those that use high price as a signal of quality. The work we do and the way we transact is a story and a signal, not simply an exchange of goods.

When you advertise your slippers on late-night TV via a toll-free number, you're probably attracting a less informed and less demanding customer, but you might be pushed by the economic demands of the medium to make bigger claims and cut more corners.

If you're a freelancer listing your work online on Upwork, you've signed up for short-term customers most concerned with price. You could have the same skills and build a very different project working for a few long-term customers in town.

We often get stuck in a customer loop, dancing ever faster for the customers we have instead of spending time and resources replacing these folks with the customers we'd like to have instead.

The best way for a freelancer to succeed is to find better customers. Better customers that pay more, demand more, and spread the word as well. Better customers aren't always easy to find, which is why the more common and convenient approach is to take what you can get.

You can choose your customers, and train and reward the ones you'd like to keep. By rewarding some behaviors over others, by keeping some promises but not making others, by having standards, you get the audience you deserve. Some things you can train customers to do:

- Be respectful (or rude)

- Be patient (or selfish)

- Keep their satisfaction to themselves (or share it with others)

- Demand personal service

- Be impatient for the next revision

- Be cheap (or generous)

- Expect pampering (or be grateful for whatever they get)

- Demand free (or seek luxury)

- Be eager to switch brands to save a buck (or be loyal)

- Be skeptical (or trust your judgment)

The customers you pay attention to—and those you fire—change the way you spend your days (if you're not firing customers, you're surrendering your future to whoever walks in the door).

You can identify and reward the customers you'd like to spend your days with. You have the freedom and power to do this if you choose.

It's not easy to persuade someone to want what you want.

It's much more productive to find people who already want to go where you'd like to take them.

112. CHOOSE YOUR COMPETITION AND CHOOSE YOUR FUTURE

It's not surprising that Lance Armstrong cheated. During his career, at the highest levels of bike racing, it was impossible to win without doping.

Everyone else is doing it.

When there's scarcity, competition ensues.

And if you choose a competition where the most successful path is short-term thinking and a race to the bottom, you've decided how you will spend your time.

113. CHOOSE THE SOURCE OF VALIDATION AND CHOOSE YOUR FUTURE

Who are you seeking to please?

Is that validation directly in alignment with how you are rewarded and how you're organized?

Cracker Barrel isn't trying to please the food critic at the *New York Times*.

They're consistent and coherent about who they are for, and how pleasing that community advances their goals and rewards them.

Reading the reviews, pleasing the critics, listening carefully to the loudest and angriest customers—these are strategic choices. If they're helping your project reach its goals, embrace them.

Many organizations, though, frequently encounter stress due to a mismatch. They might be better off shunning the non-believers.

When we match where we seek validation to the work we hope to do and the rewards we hope to receive, our strategy is in alignment.

114. CHOOSE YOUR DISTRIBUTION AND CHOOSE YOUR FUTURE

Distribution is the act of bringing the thing you make to the people who want it. Distribution is harder to visualize, but ultimately is just as important as the other choices you make.

Should you put your audio interview show on the radio, on a podcast, or on a CD? Or should you only perform it live at the local community center? The conversations might be the same, but the distribution choices will put you in different systems, create different pressures, and result in different rewards.

Venture capitalist Mitch Lasky has highlighted how important this is for video game companies, but it affects every organization seeking to make an impact.

FTD changed the flower business by changing how the flowers were distributed—the growing didn't change, the flowers didn't change, but the florist industry changed.

Steam transformed the video game business by helping game developers leave CDs and floppy disks behind.

Taskrabbit changed how the hard-working folks who lift furniture and assemble it spend their days. The assembly is the same, but the source of customers, the interactions and the process have all been transformed.

Apple determines not only the marketing but the actual design of apps that are built to be distributed in their app store. An app isn't different from a website just for technical reasons. It's also constrained and enabled by the way it is distributed and how that distribution changes the posture of the user.

It's not simply trading one middleman for another. When the system of distribution changes, what gets built changes as well.

115. NEWS, IDEAS, AND DISTRIBUTION CHANGES

Books were distributed in largely the same way for 400 years. Authors, printers, bookstores, and readers.

The bookstore was the powerful gatekeeper. The publishers saw the booksellers as their customers, and everything revolved around making them happy.

News was shared the same way for a century. The folks who wrote about it had a model, and the folks who made it (politicians, PR folks, etc.) acted appropriately.

And now, in the course of one generation, we share writing differently, from books to news stories.

The change in distribution has led to a change in who writes (far more people), how sophisticated and edited they are (far less), and how fast the word spreads and then fades.

And it has even changed the news itself. Many of the changes in worldwide events can be directly connected to the distribution of news.

Pick your distribution, pick your future.

116. "EVERYONE" IS ELUSIVE

We can't have an impact on everyone. None of us can.

But that doesn't mean we can't make things better for someone.

Implied in that statement is that our strategy is going to leave someone behind, ignore folks, or even be criticized.

The need for a unanimous standing ovation is a trap.

There's a way out: The people who need you, the someone who will benefit—if you hesitate to ship the work because it might not be perfect for everyone, you're actually stealing from the someones who need you.

117. WHAT DO YOU WANT?

"What do you want?" is a tough question to answer. "What's your strategy?" is one reason.

When we wonder about what we really want, insecurities arise. What if we get what we hope for and we don't like it? Or what if we fall in love with the change we seek to make and then discover we can't accomplish it?

It's easier to simply give up and give the system what it demands.

A strategy is a response to this quandary.

118. WHAT DOES IT WANT?

A useful way to understand an evolved organism or system is to ask what it wants.

What actions does it need to evoke to survive or thrive?

The flower wants bees to visit and berries want to be eaten by birds. Obviously they don't have conscious intent, but this "desire" guides their progression through the generations. When they get more of what they want, it happens more.

The same is true for manufactured objects and organizations as well.

The well-designed tool wants you to hold it by the handle, not the blade, and to use it often and safely. The successful luxury good wants you to show it off to others, and to feel a certain way when you do.

The smartphone wants your attention. As much of it as it can get, and then a little more. It does that by bringing the outside world to wherever you are, piercing the intimacy of here and the magic of now by persistently creating anxiety, generating fear, or offering satisfaction, again and again and again.

What the hospital wants is for every bed to be full—but not overfull. And for the highest-ranking doctors to feel secure in their status. And please, no iatrogenic infections or malpractice suits.

What most companies want is for the senior leadership to be well-paid and respected.

What the internet wants is for us to use it all the time, leaving tracks and traces of all of our data as we do.

In *What Technology Wants*, Kevin Kelly helped me see that the easiest way to understand how technology is changing our world is to imagine that it's another species evolving to fill and expand its niche.

When a system surprises you, it's probably because you're imagining that it wants what you want, or it wants what you want it to want.

But systems do what they do, no matter how much we want them to do something else.

This isn't intended to be cynical. It's a shorthand for seeing how we can work with existing systems to get what we want (or to change what they do). People deserve our empathy, and systems demand it.

At the same time, I'm not sure I completely buy into Stanford Beer's heuristic, "The purpose of a system is what it does."

The weather is a system, but rain is not the purpose of the system. It doesn't actually have a purpose, not in the way we usually use the term. The weather isn't *trying* to do anything. It simply is.

We can ask what a system wants if it helps us predict behavior or achieve our goals. But the human systems around us don't need to have a purpose, and even if they do, they rarely follow it.

It might be more accurate to say, "The system is what the system does."

It doesn't matter what you want it to do. Watch what it does and you'll understand what it is.

I'm not arguing that the system is conscious, or has explicit goals, or is run by an evil supergenius. But the easiest way to understand a system is to imagine that it might be. The sun doesn't "want" the Earth to rotate around it, but it sure acts like it does.

Systems want something. Before you engage with one, investing your time and your passion, it's worth understanding what the system wants.

Choosing to engage with things that want what we want is a powerful choice.

119. THE RUNAWAY CONDITIONS

Sometimes a feedback loop turns insatiable. And insatiable feedback loops, enabled and reinforced by the society we live in, almost always lead to unexpected side effects.

In the 1800s, the wealthy men of Europe developed an affinity for beaver hats and coats. It was a race for status, and the demand for beaver pelts quickly exhausted the local supply. The more they cost, the more demand increased. A feedback loop run amok.

This gave entrepreneurs in the United States and Canada an opportunity. John Jacob Astor committed his time and resources to acquiring and selling as many beaver pelts as he could.

In order to extract better terms from the Indigenous beaver trappers he encountered, he offered them alcohol at a discount, even though he knew that chronic alcoholism was ruining the health and family dynamics of those he offered it to.

As the demand for pelts grew, trappers went further and further into the woods, eventually remaking the landscape of large swaths of North America.

In most feedback loops, there's a built-in regulator. Extremes are leveled out and the system eventually returns to a stable equilibrium. Resilient systems abhor the unchecked insatiable node.

We don't have an insatiable desire for pizza. After a few slices, more slices eaten aren't better—they're worse. We don't have an insatiable desire for variety either. One or two shelves of pizza at the supermarket is great, but an entire aisle devoted to it feels overwhelming.

But capitalism creates the conditions to encourage an insatiable desire for more money, connecting it to status and affiliation. More money often creates a desire for more money.

The unfettered race for "more" among some people is the wildcard.

120. THINGS THAT SCALE

No matter how much the marketplace economy creates, invents, and sells, there remains an insatiable desire for some wants, things we can never get enough of.

The nexus of all of these desires is money. Money in itself is nothing, but the story of money means that it is a proxy for many things.

From the launch of the telegraph to FedEx to DMs, offering speed in travel and communication creates a tension that some can't resist. And once some parts of a networked system upgrade their speed, others do as well.

While all humans are aware of their status, many people who have achieved a form of it want to keep it, expand it, and show it off. There is a desire for luxury goods, from saddles to yachts to tickets in the front row. "I only want more than my share," has created an endless feedback loop.

Tim Wu made it crystal clear that once we have enough to survive, we go looking for convenience. People will trade almost anything once they're offered an option that enhances laziness or seems to multiply free time.

And this helps us see that what most people in most systems want is reassurance. Freedom from fear. Knowing that they're going to be okay, and that tomorrow will be okay too.

As people report feelings of alienation and loneliness, it seems as though the shortage of nurturing community is getting worse, despite the extraordinary amount of time we spend online, supposedly in connection with others. One reason is that people also crave celebrity. The myth of the influencer, the loneliness of the overlooked, the desire for connection and meaning... they all end up pushing people to share their ideas and their lives.

Most of these desires, particularly status, are insatiable. When the system rewards and encourages our desires, we often come back for even more. If you want to make a large impact, harnessing an insatiable desire is the method.

Status, safety, affiliation, and curiosity are universal and always interacting, as people around the world seek success and hope for solace.

121. WORKING FOR THE SYSTEM

A chicken is merely an egg's way of making another egg.

And a bride is simply the wedding industrial complex's way of making sure that the venue is full next week. Filled with people who might be the next bride.

Today might be going well, but resilient systems have feedback loops in place to maintain stability, and they invest in the future by creating frameworks to ensure that they'll persist.

Often, systems arise because they help us achieve our goals. But over time, the most powerful systems actually change our goals, and put us to work helping them satisfy their needs, not ours.

Systems create culture, and culture is the way a system quietly persists, creating gravity where there was none.

122. WHO IS IN CHARGE?

A concerned parent of a 12-year-old confided to me that they were worried about the upcoming thirteenth birthday festivities, particularly the intense peer pressure to invite 100 kids and spend tens of thousands of dollars.

"Resist!" I encouraged her. Her kid had a very small circle of friends, and the social drama and expense wasn't going to make anyone happy.

So why is it even an issue? It's hard to say "no" in many social settings.

Why are we on social media if it makes us unhappy, and why are we exhausted by the modern news landscape? If it's not helping us, why do it?

Because we are insatiable.

Are we a chicken? Is our only role to make another egg?

Almost certainly.

The flu virus doesn't want us to die, but it needs to make us sick so we'll sneeze on other people and spread it. Viruses that can't accomplish that disappear. The same is true for the social systems that appear to rule our lives.

But we have a chance to articulate a strategy, to choose agency instead of chickenhood. We're not here only to lay eggs to please the system.

But in most systems, most of the time, the best we can hope for is to use the system almost as much as the system is using us.

---

123. SNAPSHOTS AND MOVIES

Time isn't something we can see directly. It's simply the change in snapshots over time.

Just as a river is a lake with a current, a strategy is only possible when we consider time. As time moves forward, we find different conditions, different options, and different challenges. Our strategy is the narrative for how we will engage with our project over time.

Play all the notes in a song at once and it's nothing but noise. It's the space between the notes that makes it into music.

Now is important, but it's insufficient. Now plus tomorrow and the tomorrow after that is our project.

124. THE DAY I MET DEREK SIVERS

On June 10, 2009, I posted a riff about Guy #3, the person who starts a movement.

Guy #1 is the crazy dude who starts dancing, alone, at the outdoor concert. He's on the hillside, doing his thing.

Guy #2 is brave and supportive. He joins in and starts dancing.

But it's Guy #3 that changes the dynamic. His presence makes it safe for people 4, 5, 6, and 7 to join in.

And now, sitting still is more socially risky than getting up.

So people 8 through 20 arrive.

And now it's a movement.

We spend a lot of time glorifying Guy #1.

But the real work is to see time. To acknowledge that nothing happens all at once.

Guy #3 is the one we need to focus on.

Halfway across the world, an entrepreneur named Derek Sivers posted something about the same video on the same day. We ended up becoming friends and I published his first book. Since then, his TED talk on this topic has been seen millions of times.

But not all at once. That's the point.

125. THE EMPEROR PENGUINS, CROWDS AND FEAR

At six months old, an emperor penguin in Antarctica is ready to enter the water. Of course the water is freezing cold, but they're penguins. Most of them do it by sliding off an ice floe, probably a leap of a foot or two.

But recent drone footage from National Geographic highlights what some groups do instead.

Driven by instinct, hundreds or thousands of the penguins waddle their way to the edge of a sheer cliff covered with ice. They're forty or fifty feet above the water—a drop that would be fatal to most creatures—and these chicks are only six months old.

They crowd around the edge of the cliff, fighting their (understandable) fear of falling. Then one penguin in the group leaps (perhaps he's pushed). The others watch, astonished. After seeing the penguin swim away, a second penguin goes, and then eventually, a third.

Within minutes, the entire waddle—that's what you call a colony of penguins on the move—is leaping into the water.

They were stuck, and then they were not. But it doesn't happen all at once.

A few penguins went first.

The idea begins to spread. Peer pressure is real.

And then they're all in the water.

To be very clear: Like penguins, humans in a cultural system are herd animals.

When in doubt, look for the fear. It's probably the cause of whatever surprising behavior you're encountering.

126. IF YOU WANT TO START A FIRE

Perhaps you learned how to build a campfire as a kid.

You'll need logs, certainly.

But you will also need kindling. The bigger the logs, the more kindling. The wetter the wood, the more kindling.

Our strategy fails every time the size of the logs exceeds our supply of kindling.

127. THE FIVE STEPS TO WIDESPREAD CHANGE

It begins with a nucleus. This core group shares a desire. Perhaps they're frustrated, left out, seeking something better or something new. They are not typical.

Offer that group connection, status, forward motion, opportunity, and insight. This feeling is often different from what the masses will eventually adopt.

Second, maximize the chances for a small win. Small wins are evidence of progress. They create group cohesion, commitment, and most of all give the nucleus something to point to.

Third, give the nucleus a way to talk about the work. What they say to the others is almost certainly not what you said to them. This requires an empathic leap, offering the next circle of people a story that resonates with their desires, not yours.

Fourth, create the likelihood of another win.

This stepwise process of story » action » cohesion can be repeated again and again. Momentum is often the only thing on offer. "This is happening—are you coming?" is more powerful than, "Let me explain all the facts about what is possible."

Finally, establish new status roles, affiliation opportunities, and data exchange to codify a system going forward.

The infrastructure doesn't come first. In fact, it gets built much later, after people care enough about being part of the new system.

128. SAND HILL ROAD

Let's say you wanted to put into place a plan to get billions of people around the world to spend almost all of their time online, changing the structure of our culture and enriching a tiny group of backers and entrepreneurs.

That process started on Sand Hill Road in Menlo Park, California, about fifty years ago. Kleiner Perkins was the first venture capitalist to move to an office park there, followed by Sequoia Capital, the Mayfield Fund and Accel Partners.

They often invested less than a million dollars at a time, and their successes included Apple, Atari, and Sun. These early wins led to more entrepreneurs showing up, more limited partners offering money for them to invest, and more attention from the public markets.

The process remained the same. The actions evolved over time, and the successes led to the system that exists to this day. Not just a building, but a culture, a model, a market. The system they built was embedded into existing systems in finance, law, technology, education and more.

Now, there are thousands of VCs, all based on the model that was built and polished in one office park on one road in one town. Those original firms could all close, but the system and the culture they built would carry on without them.

129. 100 IS A FINE WAY TO START

Here's an example of how a system that's ready to shift can embrace a change.

In 1979, Lynn Taylor, a kindergarten teacher in Livermore, California, brought a puppet and a hundred pennies to class. She introduced her classroom to the concept of the 100th day of school and turned its arrival into a celebration.

The next year, she and a few other teachers successfully repeated the process.

In 1981, they published a short article in an international newsletter for teachers called "Mathematics Their Way."

Note the progression here.

The nucleus.

The small win.

An easy way to talk about the work and a way to publish it.

That small win can be repeated annually. It's safe, you're affiliated with the other teachers, and your status goes up by leading the way. If you miss the day, you can't do it later, so tension is created.

And then there are worksheets, booklets, traditions and sooner or later, it's the thing we've always done.

At every step along the way, Lynn and the movement gave the system precisely what it needed, but also altered the system along the way. According to the *Chicago Tribune*, "A true grasp of 100 is a gift, a peek behind the curtain of the magic and power of huge numbers, the key to infinity. Understand 100, and you understand 200. Understand 200, and 300 and 400 come into focus, then 1,000 starts to make sense and most of the other numbers you need to decode everyday life."

This wasn't a substantial breakthrough that transformed the system of kindergarten education forever. But it worked because it was embraced, and it was embraced because it advanced the goals of those involved.

130. FAILING TO CHANGE THE DONATION DYNAMIC

My story about kidney donation sounds similar to the challenge of improving kindergarten, but it has a different, less positive conclusion.

When a family member needed a kidney, I came face to face with the organ donation shortage. I saw that some were trying to solve the problem by moving to a new location—finding a region where they had a better chance of moving up the wait list. Another solution that hadn't gained traction was turning organ donation from opt-in to opt-out, as it is in some countries. And there were even macabre solutions bandied about, including proposing to pay impoverished families to donate a recently deceased relative's organs, which is a horrific slippery slope.

As dramatic as the stakes are here, it's still a game. There are scarce resources, allocation problems, and strategies to get ahead. The game that is played is wasteful and leads to needless trauma.

My proposed solution was to make one simple shift to the way the organ donor list was prioritized by adding a simple variable: How long have you been on the donor list?

If someone is ethically open to receiving a kidney, it follows that they should have been willing to donate one if they passed away. Most of us would agree that being willing to receive a kidney when you're alive means you ought to be willing to offer one after you're deceased.

The competitive pressure to get on the donor list early would change the conversations between doctors and patients. Doctors would have an urgent incentive to advise every patient to get on the donor list as soon as possible.

One shift in the waitlist rules had the potential to significantly increase the number of organs being donated—perhaps even leading to enough supply that we wouldn't even need a waitlist.

My friend and colleague Dr. Jonathan Sackner Bernstein worked with me to turn the idea into a paper. He's a respected medical researcher, and his skills and status helped us create a short article that was featured in the journal *Transplantation* in 2004. It was cited by the *Yale Journal of Health, Policy and Ethics* a year later. And then progress in changing the rule mostly stopped.

How did this differ from the lighter problem of spreading the 100 days of kindergarten idea?

Kindergarten teachers have a large amount of freedom in how they schedule their day. Many of them are open to new ideas and they don't need to go to a meeting to try them out. The early adopters in this audience were eager and receptive.

The top tier of professionals working in transplantation and public policy don't really match this description. They want proof. They don't want to make a mistake. And most of all, they don't want to go to thousands of meetings with angry folks defending the status quo. So they leave things as they are.

The biggest challenge to our proposal was that there were no small wins available. While it makes logical sense, it's not like this idea could work in a few towns and then spread like a dandelion, popping up here and there. It is either in place across the system or it's not.

And the other challenge is that Jonathan and I didn't spend five or ten years committing to the spread of the idea. We didn't speak at one conference after another, seek out grants for more detailed studies, and most of all didn't confer status on highly leveraged individuals who would benefit by further spreading the idea.

Good ideas are required, but they're rarely sufficient.

131. SHUN THE NON-BELIEVERS

As an idea moves through a community, some of the early adopters who join in early are aligned on mission and eager to help it succeed.

But most of the people we encounter are skeptics. They're looking for an easy way to keep things the same. They're uncomfortable with the tension that change brings, and will conceal that fear with objections that seem like thoughtful feedback.

It's not.

If a change is gaining traction with the nucleus that can move it forward, a difficult but essential part of our leadership is to ignore everyone else.

Ignore the thoughtful commentary, the shortcuts on offer, and the chance to impress a powerbroker by changing what you do.

Do this with respect, of course. Forgive people who don't get the joke. It's not for them.

You'll have time to water down and broaden your idea later.

The hard work isn't to appeal to everyone. The hard work is to get out the vote, to get the folks who want the change you want to show up, persistently and generously, over and over.

132. UNDERSTANDING ADOPTERS

Can you imagine a bell curve? It's the standard hump in the middle that we see in statistics all the time.

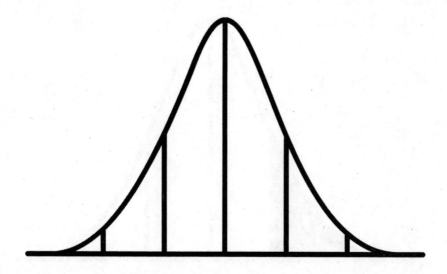

Measure the height of every person in my town, and you'll discover that about two-thirds of the people are grouped in the middle, between five and six feet tall. Moving left, 10 to 15% are less than five feet tall, and all the way to the right, another 15% are taller than six feet.

So far, so good.

Everett Rogers blew this curve wide open when he realized that instead of height, we could put time on the bottom axis.

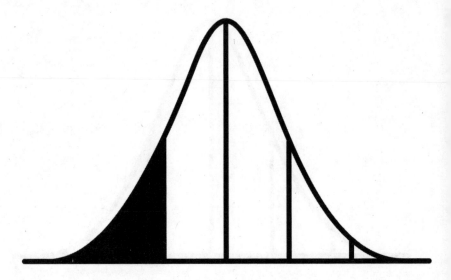

At the beginning, only a few people—the early adopters—are interested in a new thing (the part highlighted in black). Tomorrow, they might tell a few more people. In a month or a year or a decade, the number of people who will be the next to embrace this idea is represented by the hump in the middle of the curve, and then, finally, years later, it has moved its way to the end. Most people are in the middle, and most people don't go first.

Almost no one had email in 1976. Almost no one bought a Mac in 1984. Almost no one bought an iPhone on the first day.

The first group are early *adopters*, not adapters. They're eager. They're looking for something new. Their role in the system is to bring innovation, and they gain status and satisfaction by looking for something better.

This is less than 3% of the population. That means that when you bring something new to the world, 97% of the folks you interact with will not embrace it.

The folks at the far end of the curve are *adapters*. They fight change. It's a threat to them. Adapters have plenty of objections, but what they're really saying is, "I'm afraid."

Anthony Iannarino teaches that that the job of a sales team isn't to persuade people to buy from us. It's to find the people who WANT to try something new, and to politely and eagerly send everyone else on their way.

The job of the marketer is to make something so remarkable that this tiny group of adopters can't stop telling their peers. They're the ones that get the word out, not you. This phenomenon has been clear for decades, and yet people keep looking for a shortcut.

A shortcut to change the entire system.

A shortcut to promote an idea to every human and explain why the new way is better.

A shortcut to get picked.

Your idea might be rejected because it's not better. But it's probably going to be rejected because it's new.

133. TIME IS THE OVERLOOKED AXIS

Does sticking with a diet help you lose weight?

Perhaps. But not today. Maybe eventually.

Does launching a breakthrough new product change the culture and deliver a profitable return?

Perhaps. But not today. Maybe eventually.

We can draw curves all day long, but most people will hesitate to truly grapple and understand them. We pretend we do—we nod our heads about the product adoption lifecycle, or at the growth in carbon emissions, but we're humans, largely living in a three-dimensional world. There's left and right, up and down, and forward and back.

But that's not what the graphs actually show us. They show us the fourth dimension—time.

It's not really one graph. It's actually a tall stack of graphs: a graph for yesterday, another for tomorrow, and on and on. One newspaper shows us what happened yesterday. But if we read 3,000 of them, we understand what happened over a decade.

Time and systems hide in plain sight. The systems of today are often invisible, and tomorrow is an unexplored and undiscovered land.

A strategy requires us to travel through time—to get from today to tomorrow and the tomorrows after that.

134. GETTING COMFORTABLE WITH A SERIES OF SNAPSHOTS

And then what happens?

We put up a YouTube video and the seven people we send the link to see it.

And then?

One of them shares it with three people.

And then someone sends it to their joke-a-day list and now it's a thousand views.

Or perhaps they don't and it slowly fades away.

Every one of these steps are points along the adoption curve. Something happens and then something else happens (or doesn't).

135. EMBRACE THE GULF OF DISAPPROVAL

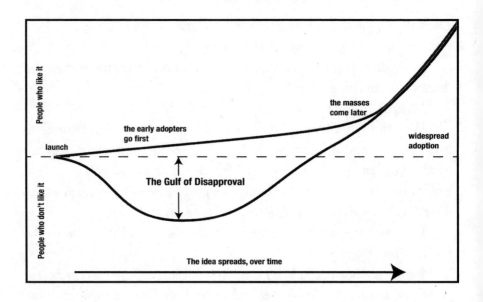

As your new idea spreads, most people who hear about it will dislike it.

Starting at the left, your new idea, your proposal to the company, your new venture, your innovation—no one knows about it.

As you begin to promote it, most of the people (the bottom line) who hear about it don't get it. They think it's a risky scheme, a solution to a problem no one has, or that it's too expensive (or some combination of the three).

And this is where it would stop, except for the few people on the top line. These are the early adopters and believers—and some of them are sneezers. They tell everyone they can about your new idea.

Here's the dangerous moment. If you're keeping track of all the people who hate what you've done, you'll give up right now. This is when the gulf of disapproval is at its maximum. This happened to the telephone, to the web, to rap music. Lots of people may have heard of it, but the number of new fans (the top line) is far smaller than the number of well-meaning (but in this case, wrong) people on the bottom line.

Sometimes, if you don't give up, the value created for the folks on the top line begins to compound. And then those fans persist, and one by one they convert some of the disapproving masses. Person by person, those you seek shift from being skeptics to accepting the new status quo.

When the gulf of disapproval comes, don't track the non-believers. Count the top line instead.

136. DETERMINISTIC NONPERIODIC FLOW PROVES THE POINT

Edward Lorenz wrote a scientific paper in 1963, publishing it in a respected scientific journal for meteorologists. The chart below chronicles how many other papers referred to his through the years.

1963-1973: A few citations per year

1974-1989: Steady growth, reaching several hundred cumulative citations

1990-1999: Accelerating growth, reaching a few thousand cumulative citations

2000-2022: Rapid growth, reaching 10,000+ cumulative citations

His paper is considered the foundation of chaos theory, and it's been referenced in almost every area of scientific scholarship.

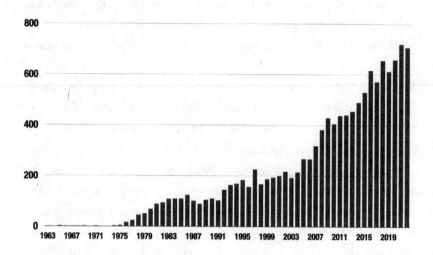

Was the paper a failure when it was published? When did it become a success? What changed about the paper itself over the sixty years as it spread through the community?

Ideas that spread, win. And traction is underrated.

137. CHASING THE HYPE CYCLE

In 1995, Jackie Fenn developed the Gartner Hype Cycle. It's not a cycle at all, but instead highlights, as Rogers' curve did, how an idea spreads through our culture.

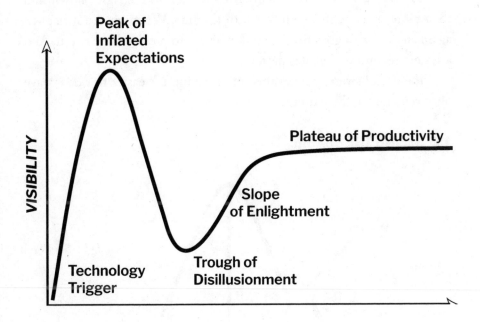

While the widespread applicability of the Hype Cycle has been debated, it's a perfect tool to help us see the role of time in culture shifts.

At the start, a new idea, technology, or fashion is introduced. This is a spark, a trigger for discussion. But on the first day, almost no one is discussing it (because it's the first day).

If hype is present, a discussion begins. The fashion gets mentioned by early adopters and media. It shows up at conferences and is shared by neophiliacs eager to gain status by being first.

If this turns into a cascade, soon it seems to be everywhere. This is NFTs, or Uggs, or any other fad you can mention. The peak of inflated expectations can only happen because of time. Like a wave that can only exist if there's an ocean, this cascade represents the amplified and connected voices behind it.

The Humane AI pin generated enormous hype and expectation, collected hundreds of thousands of preorders, and surfed on the peak of inflated expectations. Those expectations were so high that the momentum crashed and burned, leaving the future of the product in shambles.

You can feel the wave moving from the left to the right, slowly and then more quickly, and then out with the tide. When we see it happen again and again, it goes from a random event to predictable pattern. And a system relentlessly creates patterns.

The useful strategy takes this into account. It's easier to ride a wave once you can see the pattern.

138. SEEING THE CHASM

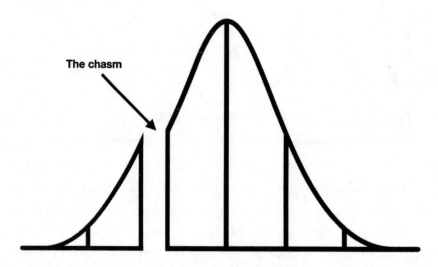

Geoff Moore took Rogers' idea and expanded it by focusing on the way time unfolds as an idea spreads through the culture.

While it's true that the innovators and early adopters are a small group, eager to go first, they rarely influence the early majority.

There's significant affiliation and cohesion among people who lead the culture. They find status and reassurance when they're in sync with one another. One person starts listening to a new song or wearing a new designer or using a new form a tech, and quite quickly, a community is all doing it.

And then, most trends stop. They hit the chasm.

This is the moat between culture innovators and the masses. The culture innovators prefer to go first, while the masses prefer the status quo.

The change we seek to make will encounter the chasm. When it does, the system, defender of the status quo, will work to keep it there. How? Through policies, hesitancy, and fear, along with skeptics, price shoppers, and those in search of convenience.

Your non-profit might not get funded by the foundation. Your important policy won't get a fair hearing from the government. Your internal innovation won't be adopted by the bosses.

It's not personal. It's what the system does to remain in force.

Absolutists and extremists often are swallowed by the chasm. So are dedicated social activists and people seeking urgent and important change. The fuel for this selfless work is often based on an uncompromising desire to make things better. Right Now.

But the system wants what it wants, not what you want.

It's possible to have an uncompromising desire but be willing to compromise. It's possible to trade the failure of *now* for the success of traction and the magic of inevitable progress.

Nobel Prize winner Wangari Maathai started a movement that built the Green Belt and led to the planting of more than 30 million trees. But the first day, the first week, the first month, few trees were planted.

Systems problems demand systems solutions, and we cross the chasm when we create the conditions for the defenders of the status quo to eagerly embrace our movement.

139. THE NEED FOR SCAFFOLDING

You and I could climb Mt. Everest. Not the whole thing, but we might do a fine job at the beginning.

The climb to the peak of Mt. Everest is legendarily difficult, but it begins with a nine-day walk from the city of Lukla to the Base Camp. Over those nine days, climbers ascend about a thousand feet a day as they walk through forests and pastures, stopping at teahouses along the way.

The long walk not only acclimates climbers to the altitude, but creates momentum and amplifies the feeling of commitment. The sunk costs are real—almost no one gives up on day ten. In fact, the tightly packed line to make the final ascent to the peak can now last for hours.

Other mountains might begin with a much steeper ascent, making them less accessible, even if they're not as difficult. Someone arrives, sees a cliff, and goes home.

Scaffolding is the cultural and organizational support we get at the beginning of adopting a new idea or practice.

The city of Lukla is scaffolding. It's a socialized, attainable, popular first step.

How can we possibly get people to save for their retirement or vaccinate their kids? Like many important and beneficial practices, they don't pay off right away. The path begins with fear or discomfort, and only later rewards us.

The scaffolding for these changes is peer support. It's the desire for affiliation. The status that comes from going first, from being thoughtful about the future, from the reputation and peace of mind that comes with being a good parent.

Lev Vygotsky described scaffolding a hundred years ago in his work on child development and learning. He introduced the concept of the "Zone of Proximal Development" (ZPD). The ZPD refers to the distance between what an individual can do without help and what they can do with guidance and encouragement from a skilled partner.

It's much easier to ride a bike if someone on Rollerblades is scooting along beside you, holding the handlebars. A few hours later, you can't remember ever not knowing how to ride.

Scaffolding is multiplied when we add cultural cohesion, interoperability, and the network effect. When we're surrounded by people who already know, our journey gets easier, and the tension involved in moving forward outweighs our fear.

When you start out, you'll need scaffolding. But the powerful application of this idea is realizing that you can offer it to others. If the change you make depends on others joining in, making that compelling and easy to do is your first and only job.

If you seek to make systems change and you haven't built the scaffolding for others to join you, it's unlikely you'll succeed.

140. SCAFFOLDING AND MARKETING

This gives us the chance to re-imagine our task as marketers. It's not about getting the word out. It's not about hustle or hype or promotion or hoopla.

Marketers build scaffolding.

We create the conditions for people who want to go where we're going to join us. We use tension and status and affiliation to help people get from where they are to where they seek to go.

What's the user experience like? What's the story behind the story? And what will I tell the others?

A brand isn't a logo. It's an invitation and a promise, an expectation about who someone can become, and what the journey will be like.

141. THE CATCH-22 OF LEVERAGED SYSTEMS

"The system will adopt you once you're successful.
In order to be adopted, you'll need to be successful."

If your brand is selling a lot of units, you'll get shelf space at the store. Of course, the only way to sell a lot of units is to have shelf space.

Sometimes we can use money as scaffolding. We can invest early, build assets, do promotions, and create the momentary momentum that's needed to get long-lasting momentum.

But this can be overwhelmingly expensive. It turns out that traction is the more resilient path.

The smallest viable audience engages long before the powerful nodes of the system do. We offer them something productive and delightful, and open the door to more status and affiliation.

We overinvest in this tiny group, creating a scaffolding around their experience that others are eager to join in on.

Author adrienne maree brown encourages us to move at the speed of trust. Critical connections are more important than critical mass. The next step isn't to host a huge rally. It's to create the conditions for just enough people to come back again and again and again, forming the nucleus for real change.

142. TREATING DIFFERENT PEOPLE DIFFERENTLY

A new idea needs more scaffolding than a proven one. The innovators will be people who like to go first, and they often seek to feel smart by figuring it out on their own. Pioneers, out in the desert with nothing but a pocket knife and a soldering iron, heroically making it work.

They'll eagerly tell their peers, a way of raising their status by humble-bragging about how smart and brave and innovative they are for going first.

The next group, the early adopters, are happy to be early, but they don't want to feel dumb, particularly next to their innovative friends. These folks need your help. The scaffolding you provide them will help them increase their competence quickly, so that they can feel affiliated with the innovators who brought them along. They'd rather not have to do their own soldering, and the sooner they experience the benefits of your idea, the better.

If you succeed in creating cohorts around the change your project makes, it's possible that the early adopters will talk to their friends and colleagues. These are the early majority, the regular folks, the people who aren't seeking change or novelty, but simply want something that works better.

If you treat this group like the innovators, you'll fail.

Not every idea or intervention makes it this far. Many innovations end up in the chasm—good ideas that didn't have sufficient scaffolding to reach the masses.

And some projects, regardless of scaffolding, never reach most people. In fact, almost all projects are in this category, and that's okay. The smallest viable audience is still viable.

143. SHIFTING TO THE MASSES

The shift from early adopters to the masses is such an essential yet over-looked concept that it's worth pausing for a moment to see it all around us. As a project spreads through a community, it develops into a complete solution, with convenience, reliability, and utility driving forward motion.

The original personal computers needed to be assembled and pro-grammed with switches. They now fit in your pocket, understand speech, and reward laziness.

Frank Zappa's early recordings weren't nearly as popular or accessible as the novelty hits at the peak of his commercial success. His early work was only for cerebral fans. The novelty songs delivered exactly what they promised to less-involved listeners.

The original bean-to-bar chocolate from Scharffen Berger was first sold in three-pound blocks for chefs at one farmer's market. Now it's sold by Hershey's in a snack pack.

Purists still use analog Nikon cameras and develop their own film. Everyone else takes billions of pictures a day with a click on a phone.

Yet there are far more projects that don't move horizontally to reach everyone. Good work, created by people who are embracing a particular audience.

Kamasi Washington makes extraordinary music. His jazz records are adored by critics and serious listeners, but you're not hearing him on pop radio.

Apollonia Poilâne doesn't compromise her bread to make it cheaper or easier to get or to have more shelf life. And yet some people fly to Paris from all over the world just to buy a loaf.

The masses are a choice, one you can commit to or plan on avoiding.

144. MISUNDERSTANDING QUALITY

The common colloquial understanding of "quality" is some combination of perfection and luxury. With this view, a Rolls Royce is a higher-quality car than a Toyota Camry.

This isn't a useful definition of the word.

According to Deming and Crosby and other quality pioneers, quality simply means "meets specifications."

By that definition, the Camry is actually a higher-quality car. It doesn't vary from one car to another. It doesn't break down. It is exactly what it said it was going to be.

When we pursue quality, we then have two jobs:

- Agree on the spec for the customer we seek to serve.

- Make sure the product or service meets the spec.

An early adopter, someone eager for the newest model and latest style, doesn't care so much about every seam matching up or whether or not the testing is complete. They actually prefer a different spec—the spec of soon and new and now—even if it's rough compared to what it will be.

The user in the middle prefers a spec where price and performance are in balance. They want something proven, something convenient, and something inexpensive.

And the laggards, those that are going last, prefer cheap and boring most of all.

As time passes, the spec changes.

Perhaps your definition of better doesn't matter. We can use someone else's version of it and set the spec accordingly.

145. THE CHALLENGE IN FINDING USEFUL CRITICISM

Prototypes are rarely applauded by amateurs.

Show a typical car owner an early model of a new car design and they'll focus on all the parts that don't work and the challenges in fit and finish.

I've learned over time not to ask for critical editing and opinions on early drafts of books or projects. Certainly not from people who mean well but haven't learned to give useful advice as a professional.

This isn't a criticism of someone who is interested and is generous enough to care. It's simply a mismatch.

Useful early criticism is grounded in an understanding of time. "This tree is too small" isn't helpful, because the gardener already knows the tree is going to grow.

Useful advice accepts that time will do its work. The creator knows that. The real question is: How do we make the spec better?

We're not asking if you like it. We're asking, "For the kind of person we seek to serve, given that time will improve many of the elements you see, what's missing?"

146. BEING CLEAR ABOUT "BETTER"

It seems pedantic to have a discussion about "better," but it's actually at the heart of your strategy.

Better for who?

Does better mean cheaper, faster, more resilient, more sustainable, higher status, more connected, more convenient, more expensive, tastier, healthier, funnier, shorter, longer, heavier, lighter, or more highly recommended?

When we lack the empathy to imagine someone else's "better", we're on the road to frustration.

147. WHAT WE ASK OURSELVES WHEN IT'S OUR TURN ON THE CURVE

We each have a choice. As customers or citizens, workers or purchasing agents, we stand wherever we like on the adoption curve over time.

Perhaps you're an early adopter (for tech, or fashion, or cosmetics). Perhaps you're a laggard, waiting until you have few options and plenty of pressure to get on with it.

Some people are attracted to the latest discussions about molecular biology but buy the same peanut butter every single week. Others are impatient for the next hip restaurant but wear exactly the same style of shoes every single day.

Wherever you choose to stand, it's likely you're asking yourself go/no go questions.

Writing about technical change, Rogers has outlined the questions that inform any cultural or economic change we seek to make. I've added a few based on a strategic and cultural mindset. It takes empathy to answer these questions with others in mind, but it's essential.

Engineering and performance

- How does this innovation improve on previous solutions?

- What are the benefits of using this innovation?

- Can the improvement be measured in terms of cost, speed, efficiency, or other metrics?

Interactions and network effects

- Does this innovation align with the smallest viable audience's values, beliefs, and current needs?

- Is it compatible with existing systems, practices, or technologies already in use by the target audience?

- Will it work better when more people use it?

- How does the innovation fit into the social and cultural context of the audience?

Convenience and simplicity

- How easy is the innovation to understand and use?

- What is the learning curve like?

- Are there any complexities or technicalities that could hinder its adoption?

Risk reduction

- Can the innovation be tested on a limited basis before a commitment to full adoption is made?

- Is it possible to pilot the innovation with a small group or segment of the target audience?

- How easily can trial results be measured and analyzed?

Scaffolding

- Do new users get status or organizational benefits?

- Are the results of using the innovation visible and apparent to others?

- How can success stories or benefits be demonstrated or communicated to potential adopters?

- Do existing users bring tension to those that might be holding back?

---

148. SHORT-TERM AND LONG-TERM GAMES

Our interactions with other people and the systems they are part of can be seen as games. A short-term game is a discrete interaction with an outcome. Some examples:

- Talking your way out of a traffic ticket

- Finishing a freelance project and pleasing the client

- Writing a post that wins a lot of attention online

- Winning an argument with your partner

A long-term game is the sum of a series of short-term games. Examples include:

- The outcome of a night of playing poker

- A ten-year career as a brand manager

- Building a platform for your work online

Luca Dellanna reminds us that winning all the short-term games is not the best strategy for long-term success. He proposes a few ways to consider a series of games. Here are three:

- Use short-term games to build long-term soft assets like trust or habits.

- Play iterated games, embracing the fact that you'll probably be back tomorrow.

- Take intentional risks, but don't expose yourself to the chance of losing your core assets.

You might lose a short-term game but lose in a way that makes it likely you'll be invited back. No tantrums, no bridges burned.

A successful strategy lines up games with intent, seeking out the sorts of interactions that build over time instead of waiting for the phone to ring and doing whatever the world decides is next on your agenda.

149. INFINITE OR FINITE?

There are infinite and finite games.

Finite games are games we play to win. They have players, beginnings, and endings.

Infinite games are games we play to play.

A wrestling match is a finite game, and so is an election. A game of catch with your nephew is an infinite game. We don't seek to win at catch—we just want to play it.

James Carse helped us understand that there are always games within games, and that focusing on the infinite games of contribution and connection is a worthwhile way to live.

In the realm of finite games, some are based on abundance, others on scarcity. An election is a scarcity game. There are winners and losers, and the only way for you to get a vote is to take it from someone else.

There are entire industries that are based on scarcity. Farming is about increasing yield on a finite piece of land. Network TV is about gaining market share at the expense of other broadcasters.

But there are also finite games that involve abundance. Book publishers understand that one book rarely competes with another—the opportunity is to sell more books overall. Bookstores are filled with competitive titles, but that's where books sell best—next to other books.

Every strategy includes a game. We need to choose and understand the game we're playing.

150. SCARCITY OR ABUNDANCE?

If you want to win the gold medal in bobsledding, you'll need to beat every other team. This is a scarcity game where the winner takes all. No medals for fourth place.

Real estate brokers profit from scarcity. When six people want the penthouse apartment, only the person who pays the most gets it.

Entering a system that is built on a particular sort of scarcity requires your project to produce more value than the existing solution does. Solar panels are easier to sell when they can produce electricity for less money than coal can. The cash is scarce, the need for electricity is real, and the benefit is clear.

In most models of economics and in most versions of our day-to-day strategy, scarcity is at the heart of the game. Only one person can get this job. Only $300 will be spent today on accommodations. Only one movie can be watched at a time.

Copyright is based on scarcity, as are luxury goods. If everyone had access, it wouldn't be worth much.

But there's been a remarkably swift increase in games that are based on abundance instead.

Networks built on information or connection abhor scarcity. They're built to be generative instead.

The kidney proposal and the 100 days idea are generative. They don't take anything away from anyone—instead, they produce value where there hadn't been value before.

Generative approaches create value. It's a chance to trade abundance for scarcity.

We've generated 7 billion jobs in my lifetime. It turns out that productive enterprises often produce the conditions for more productive enterprises.

Ideas that spread win. When connecting people, 2 + 2 can actually end up equaling 7. That's one reason why the internet has grown so fast— the network effect pays dividends to everyone participating.

It's easy to get confused about which sort of game we're in, since scarcity and abundance often work in opposite ways. When we go against the trend and trade one for the other, surprising things often happen.

151. DOMINANCE OR AFFILIATION?

There are games that are won by dominance and those that are won by affiliation.

For example, if you want to be the most successful doctor in town, you don't do that by dominating the other doctors. Instead, you do that by affiliating with them. Referrals come from people who trust you, not those who have been beaten by you.

On the other hand they're plenty of games we play where the way to win is by dominating an opponent (even thinking of the other party as an opponent is a clue).

It's not only pro wrestling. Chefs in old-school French restaurants dominated their employees to ensure obedience, and many corporate cultures are built around market share and property rights, not community or the network effect.

Retail shelf space is scarce. The way brands win is by dominating the shelf. They do this by increasing sales per square foot of their products so that merchants will stock more. They further this advantage by paying retailers up front for ever more shelf space, and then investing in promotions and advertising. More shelf space supported by more ads leads to more profit for the retailer... which leads to more shelf space.

All the merchant cares about is which brand is going to return the most profit per square foot. They don't need or want to like your product, nor do they need or want to care very much about how hard you're trying.

If you're not ready to play a game based on dominance, don't start.

152. PAYING IT FORWARD VS. PAYING IT BACK

Paying it back is trading favors. Reciprocity is a natural human instinct, amplified by culture. If someone does a nice thing for you, you are inclined to do a nice thing in return.

Paying it forward means offering something to someone who can do nothing in return for you.

This act of feeding the culture isn't focused on what you'll get back today. It simply creates the conditions for the culture to pass it on.

In some Indigenous cultures of the Pacific Northwest, such as the Kwakwaka'wakw, Haida, and Tlingit, the tradition of potlatch arose. The term is loosely translated as "to give." A potlatch is a ceremonial feast that involves the redistribution of wealth and gifts to demonstrate the host's status, prestige, and generosity within the community. During these ceremonies, the host would give things away, including food, clothing, and other valuables. In some extreme cases, the host might give away so much that they would be empty-handed and naked.

In addition to demonstrating status, potlatches also served to reinforce social hierarchies and relationships between different families and clans within the community.

The miser, on the other hand, is sufficiently insecure that he won't even open the door for a stranger. They are trapped in protecting what they have, neither paying anything forward nor back.

153. MAINTENANCE, SUBSTITUTION, OR POSSIBILITY?

The maintenance game preserves the status quo. It's the fourth *Dune* sequel. It's just enough customer service to a contractor's HVAC clients that they don't go looking for another vendor. It's keeping the classic dishes on the menu so you don't alienate the regulars.

Department stores play this game. They're defending their real estate and their leases. In fact, most traditional organizations embrace sunk costs and play to not lose what they've got.

A substitute-and-improve game happens when an insurgent promises customers what the incumbent offers, but better. Successful substitutes create tension, creating the conditions so that people who stick with the original risk losing status and affiliation. The substitute offers a combination of fear (of missing out) and status that persuades those who might otherwise stick with the status quo.

And possibility? This is the game of betting on the future. It's often a more difficult leap—this new thing isn't the complete solution. It may feel risky, but it's exactly what the early adopters want. This is a promise of better, soon. The early adopters don't ask for proof, but something to believe in.

154. GAMES OF SKILL, LUCK AND PRIVILEGE

Some games are won because systems, strategy and circumstances favor one player over the others. Other games are simply based on luck.

Systems of caste and privilege stack the deck against many. Historical and current cultural and economic biases tilt the game and cost us all in terms of dignity and productivity. Together, we need to work to make these games more fair.

In many places, though, we have the chance to play games of skill. These games reward preparation, strategy, and effort, along with talent and access to assets.

It seems obvious, but it's not: If you're interested in developing your own resilient path, focus on games that are based on skill—and go get those skills.

155. GAMES WITH DIVERGENT OBJECTIVES

In the common understanding of games, things like organized sports and other competitions, it's assumed that all the players want the same thing.

Only one billionaire can have the most money or power. Only one sprinter can have the fastest time.

But the players of most games in the real world are often seeking different outcomes. This is why it's possible to resolve many interactions with a win-win scenario.

The restaurant owner wants to increase productivity and have as many seatings a night as she can. The local diner might be willing to eat really early in exchange for achieving a different goal, which is avoiding crowds while also paying much less for dinner.

Our opportunities multiply once we see that other nodes in the system might not want what we want, and perhaps we can trade so that instead of being in opposition, we can become partners.

We'll need to seek out these games before we start imagining the win-win solutions that can transform a system.

156. MUTUAL ENROLLMENT AND COMPLEX GAMES

Chessboxing works because the players agree on the rules (the rules are ridiculous—you can look them up). Once you're in the ring, you can implement a reliable strategy that alternates between trading rooks and trading punches. I'm suggesting that you probably shouldn't chessbox as a matter of principle, but you should *definitely not* chessbox with someone who isn't signed up to do so.

Most of the time, the games we play aren't clearly marked as games, and not all the players have agreed on the rules. And most of the time, the other players may have different goals, tactics, and approaches than we do.

Consider six heirs contesting a will. One person might want to find closure as quickly as possible, accepting less than they would get if they fought bitterly. A sibling might prioritize every member of the family feeling heard and respected over a quick settlement. A third party might only care about making sure one of the other siblings (the one who always let mom down) gets absolutely nothing. And another might simply be in it for the fight, avoiding anything that feels like it might lead to closure.

In most parables of negotiations, there's a king, like Solomon, dictating the rules, or a set of clearly understood boundaries, which all parties must respect.

The hard work actually happens *before* the parable begins. "Let's get real or let's not play." The negotiation is often about how the negotiation is going to unfold. This is one reason why arbitration is such a powerful tool—agreeing to it assures mutual enrollment in the process and the outcome.

Without mutual enrollment, it falls apart. The quicksand shows up when you skip the essential pre-negotiation and assume that this system will play by the rules you're hoping for. It's a mistake to assume that each player is going to imagine the same rules.

157. DON'T BET ON GAMES YOU CAN'T WIN

There's a specific sort of micro-game that has a different strategy than the broader systems games we're discussing here, but it's worth a moment to focus on.

As we've seen, some games are actually dyads involving you and one other person. No outside forces are involved, at least not in a timeframe that matters to you.

It could be the interaction at the rental car counter, your relationship with a co-worker, or even someone you pass on the highway.

In our civilized world, the vast majority of these interactions are positive and kind. But sometimes they're oppositional. The other person has decided that they can't win unless you lose (or perhaps vice versa).

Someone is trying to dominate, creating the conditions for a non-generative showdown. There is no room for compromise or a win-win solution, because the only successful outcome for the other person is that you lose. And they may be willing to bend the rules or dramatically overinvest in order to come out ahead.

The challenge is that win or lose, you probably won't thrive in the long run. What should you do instead? Pause. Use time as an ally. Find ways to influence the larger system. Or simply walk away and play a better game with a better opponent.

Teaching the opponent a lesson in this moment may cost you more than it's worth.

We can save oppositional games for the pickleball court. They don't work well in real life.

158. ALL OF OUR STRATEGIES ARE ALL OF OUR STRATEGIES

In a finite game, when the players are all playing with the same intention, selfish behavior is expected. But there's a difference between short-term selfish and long-term maximization.

We're not sitting in traffic, we are traffic. Everyone brings some sort of selfish to the games they play.

When you build houses on Boardwalk so you can raise the rent on other players, that's okay, because that's how the game works. But when we move from this make-believe model to the real world, problems can arise.

That's because each of us lives and works and thrives in a system inhabited by other people.

The short-term selfish tactic of throwing your fast food trash out the window makes sense if your goal is to have a clean car as soon as possible, and if you are willfully ignorant of the costs of your actions on others.

But it's not a useful or resilient strategy, because once it becomes contagious, everyone (including you) will pay for it.

All resilient strategies are based on expanding our circles of us and of now.

---

159. GRABBING THE LAST DOUGHNUT

When there is competition, strategy is often offered a seat at the table.

At the turn of the century I was invited to Bentonville, Arkansas, to give a talk to Walmart. They were facing competition from an upstart called Amazon. At the time, Amazon's sales were about $3 billion a year. I was surprised to see a banner hanging in the auditorium where we met: "You can't out-Amazon Amazon." The world's largest retailer had decided to walk away from what they knew would be a fight they were unlikely to win. Twenty-four years later, Amazon's revenue is 200 times what it was then. But Walmart's sales and profits have also soared.

Competing for market share, dominance or the last pastry pushes us to think urgently about the game that's in front of us.

There are several approaches to consider:

Punching down feels ungallant, but it's actually the most common approach. Using our strengths, we eliminate weaker competition by highlighting the benefits of our dominant offering. IBM kept the computer market to itself for decades. Taylor Swift keeps selling records. The market leader offers a combination of safety, skill, reliability and leverage that makes it easy for them to serve existing systems.

Punching up can be the best option for the insurgent newcomer. Going where the dominant player can't or won't go turns your smaller size and experience into an asset.

Staying in your lane is often the right strategy for a market leader facing an insurgent. In Walmart's case, management understood that shifting their financial structure, business model and focus to shut out Amazon would require that they walk away from decades of growth in markets where they were already dominant.

Cooperation is the most often overlooked option. Alliances, networks and rewiring information flow create new opportunities because value is added, not simply captured. There are actually very few zero-sum games, we simply need to use our imagination.

What doesn't work? Insisting. Trying harder. Being just like the leader, but not them.

160. SYSTEMS THRIVE, AND THEN THEY DON'T

In 1973, Leigh Van Valen demonstrated that species go extinct as a result of changes in their environment, not because they are ancient or out of steam.

Since other species are evolving at the same time, what worked yesterday to support an organism might not work today. There's a constant race for a sinecure, and even when one is found, it doesn't last.

The Red Queen Theory helps us understand why our world seems so chaotic. AOL won the internet, until Yahoo did, until Google did, until Facebook did, until TikTok did.

There isn't an end, but simply the beginning of a new game, played anew.

Our strategy will work until it doesn't.

Because our strategy has an impact on the system, the system changes. Not simply as the result of our work, but in response to other strategies as well.

When Alexander Graham Bell offered the telephone patents to Western Union, they turned him down, because they had a perfect strategy—running a consistent telegraph business was their mission. They'd still be doing it today if the change agent hadn't arrived and rewritten the rules of the game.

Years later, when AT&T failed to capitalize on all the innovations in telecom, from fax machines to the nascent internet, they repeated the very same mistake that Western Union made—the mistake that enabled them to exist in the first place.

Your current success might have been hard-earned. But the future doesn't care about this as much as you do.

161. TO GET TO NEW YORK

The airline system is a miracle. No one is in charge of it, and it manages to deliver millions of people to where they're going, worldwide, all day, every day.

If you want to get from Los Angeles to New York, the best strategy is pretty simple. The system is ready for you, and if you show up on time with ID and money, there's a good chance you'll get to New York.

On the other hand, if you want to persuade an airline to start flying regular flights from Muskoka to New York, the system isn't going to make it easy for you. A few phone calls and a letter to the newspaper isn't going to make a change happen.

Most of the time, we work in the system, not on it.

But now, many of the systems we used to count on are changing.

We're still going to spend our lives inside of systems, but now, more than ever, we have a chance to change them as well.

If there's a hole in the boat, it's easy to spend all day bailing water with a bucket. Or we can take a moment to pull the boat onto the dock and fix the leak.

When we work *in* the system, all we can do is bail.

When we work *on* the system, we have a chance to make things better.

162. IF IT FITS, YOU CAN SHIP IT

Standards enable systems to connect.

YouTube doesn't care if the video you're watching is funny or not. Here it is. The container for the data and the way it's delivered have nothing to do with the content.

The transport company doesn't care if your linens clash—the container holds what it holds, and if it fits, they'll ship it.

Standards are consistent containers. They mean that we can automatically and easily accept anything that fits into that container, and this enables us to build complex and resilient systems.

We have standards for data packets, for nuts and bolts, and for legal business structures. And we also have standards for how we process people.

Each of us is inside a package. No one can know all of our thoughts, dreams, and foibles. When we show up in a package that fits the standard, we can engage with the system.

This works great if we're hoping to buy a piece of pizza. The system is there to trade $2 for a slice. It shouldn't matter who you are.

If we put ourselves into a standard enough package, we can get a job at Starbucks or find people to watch our TEDx talk.

If you want to manufacture a line of luggage for frequent travelers, it helps to make one that fits into the airline standard—it's unlikely the airlines will change their rules only for your company's luggage.

On the other hand, this standardization on package size doesn't help if the system is unfair, amplifies division, or is based on prejudice. It doesn't help if the side effects of the system are harmful. When we confront a system like that, fitting into the package might be too much to bear—we need to change the system instead of being a fungible part of it.

If someone is repeatedly rejected by a system, it's probably *not* because of who they are. It's because the package the system perceived didn't fit the standard. The system doesn't know you, it simply recognizes the package.

When that standard becomes toxic or harms our culture, it needs to be changed. That's a cultural and systemic shift. Teaching a bureaucrat or a customer service rep a lesson is pointless. They're busy processing packages and checking off boxes, and our indignant response simply wastes our time. Instead, we might need to consider doing what needs to be done or saying what needs to be said to work with the system in this moment, so we can find the resources to change the system with more leverage and urgency where it counts.

Sometimes, it's satisfying to rail at an unfair system at the place where the system engages with us, but in that moment, the system is probably not listening.

163. FEEDING THE SYSTEM

A friend asked about his niece's career path. She's spending hours every day on TikTok, developing videos and hoping to build a following.

She might not realize it, but she is working for TikTok without getting hired or paid to do so. She guesses at what the system wants and strives to deliver it.

Someone is going to win the lottery, but it's probably not going to be her.

When we sign up to feed the system, we're joining in with others who are offering a similar product or service. Plenty of alternatives with little chance to build a unique asset, which means that it's unlikely you'll be fairly compensated.

Feeding the system can be fun and it feels safe, which is why so many people do it.

It's a strategy with predictable outcomes. A reliable job might be what you're seeking. Sometimes, though, the system will sell us a dream it can't deliver, and these are the games we should avoid.

164. SCARCITY AND THE DRIVERS OF A SYSTEM

When a retail business is doing well, the store keeps 20% of the margin and the landlord gets 80%.

When it goes under, that's because the landlord got 105%.

The difference between rent and profit margin is the driver of success or failure for anyone with a lease.

They're not making any more real estate, so landlords are able to drive the system of retail, and often of housing.

One of the great chefs in New York was arguing for a rent rebate to help restaurants stay in business. Of course, that would simply lead to landlords raising the rent, because the shortage of great locations gives them the power to absorb any extra money in the system.

The flipside is also true: Over time, if the minimum wage rises, all restaurants don't go out of business. Instead, the ones that remain charge what the market will bear (which they are economically incented to do all along) and landlords don't raise the rents because the market can't absorb it. The real estate drives the system and works to maintain stability.

Facebook and Google are landlords. They're in the business of selling attention. When businesses seek to buy clicks, these media giants run algorithms and auctions to determine the highest price for the traffic they can sell. If the traffic is worth more to their advertisers, media sites raise the price on that traffic and absorb all of the extra value.

A law firm that makes $100 a click signing up clients for a class action lawsuit is willing to pay up to $99 a click to get that traffic. If they have competition, that's exactly what they'll end up paying, with Google keeping all the incremental value.

The lesson is simple: *Avoid projects where the system is organized to take all the value you create.*

165. SCALE AND MAGIC

The smallest organizations have an advantage when they create projects. With nothing to lose and few people to please, it's possible to create moments of magic. Small projects from small teams can leap forward with the confidence of knowing that they don't have far to fall.

When a project works, it's tempting and generous to scale it. Offer it to more people. Turn one successful restaurant into a chain, or a small medical practice into a much larger one.

And almost inevitably, it falters.

The only way to effectively scale magic is to create a strategy where the scale *is* the magic.

Heinz ketchup is better because it's the regular kind, the safe kind, the normal kind. That's the magic they offer. Disney is magic because it offers predictable, industrialized, mass fun. They turned that from an oxymoron to a motto. It's the place to go if you want to go to where everyone else is going.

Projects where the scale is the magic have a network effect. The more people who use them, the better they get.

166. HOW NPR LOST TO THE PODCAST

After the fact, it seems obvious: In 2012, public radio in the US had everything it needed to transform the delivery of audio information. A decade later, the internet hosted more than 2 million different podcasts, with listenership approaching 18 billion hours in 2023. NPR ended up with a tiny share of this ability to shift the culture and generate revenue as well.

Many of the most popular podcasts are often created and produced by former NPR radio employees, and the core audience was drawn from people who were already NPR listeners. They certainly *sound* like NPR productions.

Given the skill, staffing, attention and funding available to NPR, it would have been straightforward to be an early and persistent leader in this area, but they saw the opportunity and seemed to actively undermine their ability to take advantage of it. I remember spending time with WNYC leadership as we outlined the opportunity, and realizing that little would happen.

The system delivers what the system does.

The head of the nationwide network of stations has little power, because each member station controls the most prized resource: local spectrum. The network ceded decision-making power to the local stations, acting primarily as a clearinghouse for syndicated programming the stations wanted to put on their slice of spectrum. In the days of radio, the spot on the dial was your most precious asset.

The individuals running local stations saw themselves as curators. There's only one thing on the station at 3 p.m., and they get to decide what it is.

Beyond that, they were under listener pressure to continue running (and funding) the high-profile (and expensive) syndicated shows that filled those slots.

Creating thousands of new shows and promoting them felt like it would undermine the two things that were most important to them. They'd be sending people away from "their" station to start listening "somewhere else." And they couldn't possibly curate in the same way when their work would be to create many shows at once, not simply showcase only one of them.

Worst of all, the worldwide promotion of podcasts would undermine the mindset of local spectrum. If podcasts from other stations are stealing your listeners, how are you going to get credit, or add to your ability to control and create?

The ironic end result is that the technical change in podcasting led to a significant decrease in the value of each station's core spectrum, the very thing they were trying to protect.

When new technology changes the rules, old systems rarely thrive.

167. SELF-INTEREST IS SELF-EVIDENT

Each person in a system will always act in their self-interest.

That doesn't necessarily mean that they'll act selfishly. A healthy system is organized in a way that self-interest leads to behavior that's in the common good. People sign up for systems that give them what they seek, and they stay as long as their needs are being met.

Self-interested nodes (i.e., people in a system) make decisions based on status and affiliation. Decisions by nodes could involve questions like:

- Will this get me promoted?

- What will I tell my boss?

- Does this fit into our standards?

- Who has the power in this interaction?

- Is this something I'm authorized to do?

- What am I afraid of?

- Will I profit from this?

- What's the least risky choice for me?

- How do I maximize the metrics the system is looking for?

- What's the path of least resistance?

- Do people like us do things like this?

Status comes from comparing our standing and achievement to others. Affiliation is predicting whether the people we engage with will approve of what we've done.

The answers to these questions are driven by the links between and among the nodes. We're in the middle of the feedback loops, deliverables, inputs, and outputs that the links deliver (or we imagine they do).

Culture is "people like us do things like this." The links add up to a persistent and relentless reminder of culture.

If you want to predict how a system will respond to an input, begin by describing what's in the self-interest of the node you're interacting with.

168. IT'S EASY TO AVOID THE MOST IMPORTANT PART OF OUR JOB

We make decisions. All day, all the time.

And those decisions are based on our expectations, our perceptions of status and affiliation, our urgencies, our stress levels and our confidence. They are influenced by how big our circle of us and circle of now appear.

Add them all up, and we'll always do what we think is best.

That might include risking our lives to dive into a cold lake to save a stranger's life. It might include sending a donation to charity. It could involve slowing down to let someone in front of us in traffic. It's still self-interested.

The work of change-making is to help people decide that changing their actions is exactly what *they* want to do.

Not because it's important to us, but because it's important to them.

169. IT'S VOLUNTARY

The people around us make choices. Each person is part of many systems, and while the systems exert influence, there are still choices to be made.

The choices we each make are driven by our goals and needs, our fears and desires. In the context of the system. No one is fully alone, and no one is completely powerless. We exist in community, seek connection, and worry about our status, fitting in, and getting ahead.

The empathy of a useful strategy sees and respects the agency of everyone else.

170. "I WILL IF YOU WILL"

We rarely say this out loud, but often use it as a way to make decisions.

"We Are the World" is one of the bestselling songs of all time. The documentary about the making of the song outlined the strategy behind the all-night recording session that was organized to create the song.

The studio was filled with pop royalty. Lionel Ritchie, Michael Jackson, Cyndi Lauper, Bob Dylan, Bruce Springsteen, Tina Turner and even Huey Lewis were there.

In interviews, two things came across:

Almost every singer felt like an impostor, overwhelmed by the other stars in the room. Bob Dylan seemed shy and had trouble singing his lines. It's easy for us to imagine that no one else feels like a fraud, but here's proof that *everyone* did. Which leads to the question: If each singer knew that they'd feel insecure, why come?

It turns out that everyone who was there said they came because everyone else was there too. Miss this and you'll be left out and left behind.

We create value when we establish the conditions for status and affiliation to be delivered to those that seek it. Rock stars included.

171. BRINGING STRATEGY TO MARKETING

There are three steps:

- Tell a story, a true story, one that holds up. And tell it only to your smallest viable audience, the tiny group that is actually listening to you, that cares and that is among the early adopters. Create tension and urgency.

- Give this group a reason to share the story with others. Something that will increase their status, their affiliation with others, or increase the utility of supporting your product, service or cause. Give them the scaffolding to do this.

- Help them, through use or narrative, alter the story to make it theirs.

This means that strategic marketing begins by seeing the path, the way the idea spreads over time and through the community.

It requires a specific story, not simply, "You can pick anyone and we're anyone." Instead, we seek to be of service to a small group, people who would miss us if we didn't exist.

Once this group finds affiliation and status from engaging with our work, we create the conditions for them to share the story with others—but they won't tell the story that attracted them in the first place. They'll tell a different story, also true, and one that will attract their friends.

172. LIVING IN A VAN

Years ago, I produced several albums for a fledgling record label I had started.

One duo I produced were gifted musicians living together in a van, traveling from town to town and playing in small coffee shops, then moving on.

These places were the most accessible rung on the performance ladder, one step above open mic night.

I helped them understand that the van wasn't doing them any favors. If they stayed in one place for a while, they could build an audience and gain a reputation. After a short run at one place, they'd have enough credibility to headline a bigger club, building an audience that would allow them to work through the system.

The bookers at bigger clubs don't have better ears. They're simply nodes in a system, paying attention to where someone came from and whether or not they'll bring an audience along.

Starting over at zero because it's the easiest node is a trap, and yet talented freelancers do this every single day. A gig on Fiverr or UpWork might be easy to get, but if it doesn't plug you into a system that amplifies your work, it gets in the way of the change you seek to make.

173. ACORNS SOMETIMES BECOME OAK TREES

After years of research, in 1993 Apple Computer launched a groundbreaking product called the Newton. It was a huge success, selling more than 100,000 units in its first weeks. But in just a few months, Newton turned into the most public flop in the company's history.

About fourteen years later, Apple launched the iPhone. It wasn't particularly well reviewed, and only sold a million units in its first 74 days on sale. Hardly much of an improvement on the Newton.

Since then, it has sold 2.3 *billion* more units, making it the most profitable consumer product of all time.

The Newton and the iPhone had very similar results at the start—launch hype is overrated.

Nature is similar. After just a few weeks of development, the embryo of a human, an elephant, and a blue whale each weigh about as much as a poppy seed.

The future unfolds after the launch. When we embrace time and systems, the launch takes care of itself.

174. SYSTEMS HAVE MULTIPLE OBJECTIVES

What makes good airline food?

Well, it depends. It depends on what it's for, who's it for, and what your job is.

Antony McNeil makes 52,000 meals a day for Singapore Airlines. Some of them are for passengers paying as much for a seat as a small car might cost, and others go to coach passengers on a short flight.

Some of them are for vegans, and some for folks who look forward to fried carrot cake for breakfast.

But more than the passengers, Antony has to please the operations folks, who lose millions of dollars in profit if a plane is delayed because loading was slowed down.

And the flight staff, who have to juggle competing priorities and endless details while also ensuring the safety of the flight.

And the cleaning staff, who don't have the time or resources to deal with grease stains.

And the CFO, who would very much like to send money saved on carrots right to the bottom line.

A simple question like, "What's for dinner," becomes a complex problem, one with no obviously correct answer, because the system has independent variables and mutually incompatible goals.

There isn't a single solution. There are many solutions, and none of them are perfect.

175. ONE WAY TO SOLVE THE PROBLEM IS TO CHANGE THE SYSTEM

When JetBlue planned its launch as a comfortable but discount airline, their CMO, Amy Curtis-McIntyre, looked at the competing priorities and entrenched systems in the provisioning and service of food on airlines and reconsidered.

"What's it for?" gives us a lens to see the history of fine dining on airplanes. Trains, the original competition for expensive travel, had a long history of dining cars, chefs, and even the Agatha-Christie-worthy Orient Express. Matching some of these tropes made switching to air travel a safer cultural choice for many elites.

And then, once the meme was in place, airlines often chose to attract higher paying business travelers by competing on food. Even though the food wasn't very good, and even though it might not sway a customer's choice, the system perpetuated itself.

Why not abandon the system altogether?

Curtis-McIntyre decided to simply buy the most expensive snacks she could find and instruct the staff to push passengers to take as much as they liked.

Even with the luxury snack brands and the incentive to go wild, Jet-Blue still spent a tiny fraction of what other airlines were spending. More to spend on promotion or lower fares.

When you have the leverage, you can change the system.

---

176. INTEROPERABILITY

My dentist can't change the way he practices. Even if he wanted to, he's part of a system that won't make it easy.

It's not simply the regulatory and licensing boards that won't permit him to use different substances or approaches.

It's also the fact that he works with one or more dental hygienists, and they learn a vocabulary and a method that is easily transferred from one dentist to another.

And he depends on the sales reps and the manufacturers, who produce chairs and lights and devices that they need to sell to masses of dentists.

We are so entrenched in our professional systems that we don't even notice that most of our choices have already been made for us.

177. WHAT DOES THE SYSTEM RESPOND TO?

Systems are all different, but they often behave in similar ways. If we know what people are looking for, it's easier to find it.

Here are a few, many of which are rooted in Western commercial culture.

- **Reassurance:** This is the dominant one. The system wants what the system wants. And one thing it wants is to persist. If there's a way to spend time and money to ensure that everything will remain okay, to avoid the current emergency, that action relieves tension.

- **Faster:** The race for productivity continues unabated, and faster-moving ideas, devices, and processes often gain traction, usually by people who like moving faster, which means the adoption is faster as well.

- **More connected:** Since 1850, we've been wiring the world into a network. Systems are the original networks, and with increasing rapidity, systems are adopting approaches that further enmesh the nodes.

- **More convenient:** Tim Wu has pointed out that the wealthy consumer will trade almost anything for convenience. Dishwashers and one-click shopping are all part of the same spectrum.

- **Cheaper:** If all other things are equal (though they rarely are), people pick the cheap one.

- **More remarkable:** In a market filled with choices, few things are talked about. But remarkable items, by definition, are.

- **More status:** This is a form of reassurance. The system wants insiders and outsiders to profess respect and root for it to succeed.

178. THE PARADOX OF SUBSTITUTES AND UNIQUENESS

The best projects are often unique with no easy substitutes, There's no real price pressure because you're not offering a commodity. If you want this, here it is, and no one else has it.

And yet, many components of existing systems often have easy substitutes. Resilient systems gravitate to commodities because they feel more stable. "Everyone else is using this procedure, this part, this type of vendor, so we will too. And we can get suppliers to bid against each other for the lowest price."

We even see it in org charts and hiring. The org chart has boxes on it because the people who drew the chart are looking for replaceable cogs—people to fill a slot—not slots built around people.

Systems are wary of one-of-a-kind interventions. The more the status quo is prized, the more likely it is that the nodes in a system will be rewarded for going third, not first. There will be RFPs put out for bid, committee meetings, and plenty of attention on what others are doing.

But creators should recognize that when there are easy substitutes, there is little opportunity for profitable value creation and memorable storytelling.

179. COMMODITIES

We only sell a commodity when we act like we do.

Drinking water, clothing, even the source of our electricity—it's possible to bring a story along to create real value for the people we serve.

The system seeks to reduce tension by insisting we fit in and offer a commodity. That's a race to the bottom.

The successful insurgent creates tension as a response—the tension of FOMO and of networks that must be joined.

180. UNDERSTANDING GENRE

Genre doesn't mean "generic". Almost the opposite, actually.

If someone says that they're going to "a trade show," you can immediately visualize what they're in store for, even if you're not in their industry.

When you choose your genre, you're sending a message. You're choosing your customers and the expectations they bring with them. You're also choosing (at some level) your staffing, funding, and production models.

Genre is a signal that helps us be understood. We know that an airport bookstore sells books, but it's not in the same category as an independent bookstore in a small town, and our expectations are different in each case. But choosing a genre also helps us understand ourselves—the privileges and responsibilities that our choice comes with.

The innovators in every field are seen as innovators because they confounded our expectations of genre. And many of the failures that have tried to change the culture did the same thing. If it's not what we expect, the easiest thing to do is to ignore it.

One way we change the system is by subverting genre. That new thing might *look* like an ordinary experience or product, but once we experience it, it changes us in a way that we can't undo.

181. MEDIUM VS. MESSAGE

A friend asked me to review her investor deck. This is typically a ten-page PowerPoint, sent to potential investors in advance of a meeting.

In two words, "investor deck" defines the medium. It establishes who it's for, and it's not hard to deduce what it's for.

The actual output is not to get an investor. No one gets a PowerPoint by email and sends a check the next day. Instead, the purposes of the deck are:

- Demonstrate that you understand the genre, that you rhyme with what has come before, that you're not going to waste my time, that you are people like us who get funded like this. Decks aren't read—they are scanned. When I scan this, are you giving me an easy way to say "no"?

- Create tension. The tension of being left out or left behind. The tension that comes with seeing something I need to understand (but don't yet). The tension of what might be.

That's a lot to ask of a ten-page PowerPoint. Except not really. Because of all the things you can now leave out.

182. THOUGHTS ON PRICING

Price is a story, price is a signal, and price is a symptom of your strategy.

Cheaper might not be better: There's a bias in marketplace economics toward cheaper. Supply and demand curves show us that when the price goes down, demand goes up. And all other things being equal, this is true for commodities.

But all other things aren't equal. Something is only a commodity if the seller treats it that way.

Customers need a story to tell the boss and their friends. The story of "it's like last time but cheaper" is compelling and tempting. It's easy to sell and easy to tell. "You can pick anyone, and we're anyone, but cheaper."

But low price is the last refuge of a marketer who has run out of things to say.

It turns out that there are lots of demands on the products or services we sell, and the system might require a different sort of better.

Generous doesn't mean free: Generous work requires emotional labor. It means looking at the problem instead of looking away. Leaning in when we feel like hiding.

Generous work puts us on the hook, because it amplifies connection, it doesn't diminish it.

Generous work is more insightful than people expect, or more urgent or selfless. Generous work makes a difference, and often it's okay if that generous work is expensive.

The slogan of generous work can be, "You'll pay a lot but you'll get more than you paid for." And the tag line is, "I see you. And I care."

Ongoing costs are easier to ignore than immediate price: How much does it cost to adopt a puppy at the shelter?

Perhaps it's the $400 you put on your credit card. But that doesn't count 14 years of food, replacing the chewed-up cashmere duster, getting the carpets cleaned, the dog sitters and more.

Organizations and families make decisions based on price all the time. Thoughtful managers look at the cost.

At a certain point, a person's story about money is far more important than money itself: Successful strategies seek to find customers who are eager to pay money to solve their problems. If you want to find a lousy customer, find someone who has a scarcity mindset, or is more comfortable with their problem than they are in spending to make it go away.

Luxury isn't more utility—it's intentional waste: Luxury goods are items that are worth more (to some) because they cost more.

The cost itself is the benefit that is being sold.

There used to be a correlation between superior performance and price. In 1900, a Hermès saddle or a Louis Vuitton trunk was arguably better built for the work it was put to.

Today, though, a more expensive resort, bottle of wine, or article of clothing is likely not the item of highest performance. It is simply a symbol that the purchaser is happy to understand and perhaps show off. Poor performance might even be part of the value proposition. Not only can you afford to pay extra, but you can afford to pay extra and have your feet hurt as well.

Money is a story, and price is a way of telling that story.

183. STRATEGIES REQUIRE EMPATHY

Not sympathy. You don't have to agree with how any node in a system will choose to act.

And not, "If I were you," because you're not them. Only they are them.

This is the empathy of, "I don't know what you know, see what you see, or believe what you believe. And that's okay."

We can't succeed with a strategy that requires everyone else to care enough to come to our point of view. Perhaps the best we can do is to help people get to where they've wanted to go all along.

If the change is important, you'll need to find the empathy to acknowledge that the system (and many of the people in it) doesn't want what you want or even believe what you believe.

You can be right or you can make progress. It helps if you're right, but progress actually comes from helping other people feel as though they're right.

It's easier to help someone get to where they're going than it is to persuade them to go somewhere else.

184. DOROTHY AND HER CREW

How did Dorothy persuade the Lion, Tin Man, and Scarecrow to join her on the trip to see the Wizard? Did she make a case about how much she missed home?

The lesson here is worth remembering. *She created the conditions where the others could get what they wanted by joining her.*

They got to move closer to their stated goals of courage, compassion, and smarts. But more than that, she offered them status and affiliation.

The Wizard was simply a stepping-stone on the way to where they were hoping to go.

185. EVERYONE IS ALWAYS RIGHT

The system creates the conditions for our actions. And anyone who consistently takes an action is doing it because based on who they are, what they see, what they believe, and the feedback loop they're in, this is exactly the right thing to do.

Perhaps they might change what they do if they saw something else, if they received different feedback from the system, or if their status shifted.

We can show up with a story that resonates, and we can create the conditions for people to make different choices.

But we cannot easily persuade someone that they are wrong.

186. ALL PERSISTENT SYSTEMS ENGAGE WITH FEEDBACK LOOPS

Sometimes these loops maintain and stabilize a system, and occasionally they work in the other direction, spiraling away from the center and ultimately destroying it.

In 1952, Ray Bradbury wrote a short story called "A Sound of Thunder." In it, a time-traveling tourist to the distant past steps on a butterfly, and the entire future of the world is changed as a result.

While chaos theory predicts that tiny changes can lead to momentous outcomes, persistent systems persist precisely because they resist tiny changes.

So go ahead and kill the butterfly—the problems and challenges of tomorrow's world will remain unchanged.

Feedback loops can either be negative (stabilizing) or positive. Once feedback starts running through a microphone, it gets louder and more annoying, because audio feedback leads to more audio feedback. On the other hand, if someone acts recklessly in an airport, there are countless social and practical forces at work to diminish the interruption and return things to their normal state.

Negative feedback loops might be better understood as dampers.

If your living room gets too hot, the AC kicks on. If it gets too cold, the heater does. The thermostat instructs the house to counter the actions of the environment to keep things stable.

In *The Beak of the Finch*, Jonathan Weiner tells a story of how Peter and Rosemary Grant measure (to the millimeter) the length of the beaks on finches born on one island in the Galapagos. During wet periods, conditions are such that long-beaked finches are more successful at finding food, and therefore they are more likely to reproduce, so the percentage of finches with long beaks increases. But if the climate changes and there's a long dry spell, these finches struggle, while the short-beaked finches are more easily able to find the food they need. So the population shifts again. That's why there are still finches—the evolutionary response to the climate's changes keeps them from going extinct.

On the other hand, feedback loops can also cycle in the other direction, spiraling out of control. A simple example is the release of rabbits in Australia a century ago. With no predators and plenty of food, they multiplied (like rabbits) until a crisis occurred.

In our current climate situation, we're seeing what happens when the ice caps melt. When there is less ice, the amount of sunlight reflected back to space goes down, since blue/gray water absorbs more heat than the albedo effect created by white ice.

More sun absorbed means more ice melting. And the feedback loop continues....

We dance with feedback loops all day long. Sometimes, a small error compounds into a tragedy. Other times, a system we seek to change fights back, and the harder we push, the harder it seems to push back.

Before we build a strategy toward better, we need to see the systems. *Either we're working the system or the system is working us.*

187. THE WILDCARD IN EVERY FEEDBACK LOOP IS THE DELAY

We avoid putting a hand on a hot stove. That's largely because the pain feedback comes almost instantly. On the other hand, hundreds of millions of people smoke cigarettes. The response from their lungs can take decades, and the delay in feedback means that people may, in short-term apparent self-interest, voluntarily do something that harms them.

As systems become more complex, the delays magnify the complexity. It's like playing the piano wearing mittens. The delays mask what's actually happening.

Should the Federal Reserve Bank raise interest rates? It would be an easy question except for the delay. When multiple interventions overlap before the feedback arrives (and in something as complex as a world economy, they always do) it becomes more difficult to settle on a strategy.

A first step, then, is to seek to shorten the delay, to look for early signals that usually lead to later ones. More likely, though, we'll need to have a strategy that helps us navigate when the feedback from the system is slow or confusing.

188. SYSTEMS + GAMES + FEEDBACK LOOPS

When we combine systems, game theory, and feedback loops, we can begin to see how our actions influence behaviors over time.

Here are some of the precepts of strategic impact.

- **Think ahead and reason back:** When we know who it's for, what it's for, and how we hope to get there, we can start at the end and work backward for where to begin.

- **The empathy of a mutual win:** We can avoid oppositional entanglements when we choose to work with people and systems that want to win something we don't care so much about, especially when they offer us something we do care about.

- **Trust and expectation:** Follow through on commitments and threats to maintain credibility and influence others' behavior. Tension is real if we are consistent.

- **Make the consequences intended:** Consider the potential unintended consequences of your strategies, as they may lead to suboptimal outcomes.

- **Leverage information asymmetry:** Use your unique knowledge or information to your advantage, but be aware that others may be doing the same.

- **Create and shape the rules of the game:** If you choose to play in an arena where you have influence over the rules, it's more likely you will achieve your goals. Don't count on winning games that are stacked against you.

- **Manage expectations:** Experiences are largely relative. If it's better than expected, it's better.

- **Foster cooperation through repetition:** Encourage cooperation by engaging in repeated interactions and building a reputation for reciprocity.

- **All forward motion involves risk and reward:** When you spend time, money, and reputation to create tension, what are you hoping for in return?

- **Build scaffolding:** Demanding that masses of people leap is rarely as effective as creating the conditions for them to simply walk on board.

- **Require effort and expense from the early adopters:** When working with the pioneers, require effort and offer status. It's not convenient, easy, or free to go first—there's no tension in that. Embrace the effort. The appearance of risk is actually a benefit for this cohort.

- **What gets measured:** Create simple and useful metrics for status and stick with them.

- **Create stickiness:** Invest in systems that build stickiness for the believers and don't be distracted by the skeptics that push you to be a commodity.

- **Persistence:** People become what they do, so reward them for consistently showing up to do the new thing.

- **Moving forward:** Create one-way ratchets where sticking with the new approach is easier than giving up and moving backward.

- **Reinvest:** Use the resources earned from early users to invest in creating what the next segment of the curve wants.

189. EMBRACING CONSTRAINTS

Gabe Anderson blogged about the bigger hoop analogy.

NBA players don't complain that the hoop on the net is too small (a bigger hoop, after all, would make everything easier). Instead, they embrace the opportunity to focus on court speed, teamwork, or shooting accuracy.

All games have constraints. We can deny them or we can work with them.

190. WHO BENEFITS?

Systems evolve over time, and no system is perfect, but every resilient system persists because the momentum it creates makes it easier to stick with it than to walk away.

When we see who benefits from the persistence of the system, we've identified the people who will work to maintain it.

People adhere to a cultural system as long as the perceived safety and comfort in maintaining the status quo outweighs the potential risks and uncertainties of departing from it.

191. SIX SYSTEM TRAPS

Systems don't exist to please us. They may have been created for that purpose, but over time, persistent systems persist simply because they're good at sticking around. This sticky behavior can cause us real harm because we don't always understand where the leverage points are for making change happen.

Donella Meadows outlined several systems traps that help us see how they persist and what our options are if we want to make change happen. From a user's point of view, they seem like defects, but they're actually built into the system from the start.

- **Policy resistance** is the self-maintaining re-centering that feedback loops enable systems to achieve. We might try to fix the economy or end drug use or balance a budget, but the forces at work resist. Individuals in the system might not intentionally seek to sabotage a policy change, but the balanced system subverts it nonetheless. The status quo is the status quo because it's good at sticking around.

- **The tragedy of the commons** is the depletion of a shared resource because rational individuals believe they have no incentive to hold back. When all the farmers share a plot of land, each might as well let their sheep get fat, or someone else will. Things like clean air are hard to achieve because individuals acting in their self-interest often see no reason to invest to stop their own pollution.

- **Drift to low performance** is the disappointing path of comparing our low performance to others' even worse performance, and creating a feedback loop of lowering the bar. Once a neighborhood starts to be unkempt, it's likely that someone might care less and make it a bit worse, which amplifies the downward spiral.

- The **race to the bottom** is not the same as drift. This is the intentional effort of lower prices, worse service, more side effects, and less care. If low price is the last refuge of a marketer who has run out of energy, the system amplifies the lazy path.

- **Escalation** is an arms race, a price war, or a cycle of politicians outdoing themselves when it comes to lies, anger, or seeking shortcuts. Any individual caught in this dynamic is hard-pressed to reverse it on their own.

- **The rich get richer** is the compounding head start that some in unrestricted markets take advantage of. If you have money or status, you can save it, invest it, and profit from it, giving you more. The same is true for the lions in a pride—the well-fed ones are faster and stronger, and can thus catch more prey and become even stronger.

192. THE MOSES MANIPULATIONS

Robert Moses called himself a master builder. He created the conditions for the construction of an astonishing array of roads, parks, bridges, power plants, and more. The entire fabric of New York City was rebuilt during his 50-year reign.

He was also a master of strategy. He understood systems and how to take advantage of system traps and status to accomplish his goals.

But most of all, he is now known as the master manipulator. He used his strategic skills to create outcomes that those involved came to regret. By focusing on the short run with urgency, he failed to take responsibility for the long-term impact of his actions. He ended up using his power in a way that didn't benefit the people it was supposed to benefit.

Here are some of the Moses manipulations that take advantage of human nature and system traps. I am listing them here not as a manual on how to manipulate or help you maximize power, but so that we can be aware of them and use them with full knowledge that the ends don't always justify the means.

- **Stake driving:** Moses would begin actual construction work on a project as quickly as possible, often starting with driving actual stakes into the ground before he had permits or funding. This made the projects seem inevitable and more difficult to oppose or alter. Systems are often optimized to slow things down, not to undo things that are already happening.

- **Whipsawing:** He would create crises where groups with competing interests would focus on earning status against each other, having them compete to gain power by supporting his plans more than their opponents did. Losing an auction is more difficult for some than not entering it in the first place.

- **Wedge driving:** Along similar lines, wedge driving involved Moses exacerbating existing divisions among opposition groups or creating new divisions, thereby breaking down unified fronts against his initiatives.

- **Control of information:** Systems respond to information. By relentlessly limiting information, lying, or sharing different information with different nodes seeking power, Moses created the conditions where he was the only one who actually knew what was happening.

- **Start out of town:** Moses's most benign tactic was to build his power base in Long Island, where there was little competition for public space, and where the fight for power was much less fraught. Once he acquired his power, he moved into higher-stakes arenas.

- **Bullying:** Bullies always punch down. Moses would find someone who had less power than he did and demand loyalty and support. If it wasn't forthcoming, he would actively work to destroy the person's career and reputation.

- **Trading for power:** Short-term thinking is a common systems trap, which means that someone who is playing a longer game than anyone else has a significant advantage. They can make tactical or financial transactions that benefit others in the short run to obtain long-term status and control.

193. RESILIENT SYSTEMS STICK AROUND

The systems that persist have survived technological, cultural, and organizational shifts. They're good at it.

The system of markets and trade, of course, has been around for as long as there have been people who needed something.

The Bank of Sweden was founded in 1668 as a central bank, and shows no sign of going away.

The Grand Bazaar in Istanbul, Turkey, is still recognizable 500 years after its founding.

Hollywood has moved from silent films to talkies, to television and then back to summer blockbusters. It has navigated the birth of theater chains and their demise, as well as video rentals, then DVDs, and now streaming.

The system adjusts.

We can influence it, but it's unlikely we can simply replace it.

194. TRYING TO TURN ME INTO AN ADDICT

A few years ago, I found myself in the burn unit with a serious infection. It was a top-tier facility with a terrific staff.

Every four hours, they woke me up to have me take my meds. The first time, I was awake enough to ask what they had on the tray. "Yes, that makes sense," I said each time they handed me a pill, until they handed me the Fentanyl.

I said I'd prefer to deal with the pain, and explained I wasn't going to take an addictive painkiller—not now and not later.

Four hours later, it was there again.

And then again, four hours later.

I finally escalated my concern high enough to have my orders changed, and then the override system prevented them from coming back.

No one at the hospital wanted me to take a medicine I didn't want or need. But the system did. There was no systemic intent, only the effect.

195. THE CHALLENGE OF FALSE PROXIES

If you change what gets measured, you'll change what gets done.

The nodes in the system work to achieve their goals, and that effort, coordinated without a coordinator, creates the forward motion and power of the system.

How do people know what to do?

They know what they want. They want status, affiliation, comfort, freedom from fear, and convenience. But each of us is a bit unsure how to get those things.

And so we seek out proxies.

Getting into a famous college isn't the cause of satisfaction. It's a goal, an achievable proxy, a way to tell ourselves a story. The same is true with making money, avoiding a dirty look, or clearing our inbox.

The best tactic I know for someone seeking to influence a system is simple: Elevate the useful proxies and diminish the presence of the false ones.

At Google, every employee knows the stock price, and most know the quarterly earnings numbers. But if an employee's focus is on those two short-term numbers, it's no surprise if they act in a short-term way.

What if other metrics had been made more vivid and distributed widely?

Things like:

- The percentage of failed searches

- The trending sentiment of loyalty and trust in the brand

- The health of the ecosystem that the network depends on

- Impact of philanthropic ventures

- Shift in the literacy rate

- New projects built on the API

- Daily average users of email

I'm sure you can think of ten more.

196. WE SEE SYSTEMS WHEN THEY ARE FORCED TO CHANGE

For most of my lifetime, the system of book publishing and the culture change it causes has been relatively stable.

Books are launched with two lists a year, fall and spring. The reason is that they used to travel to stores from New York via the Erie Canal, and the canal froze each year, making shipments in the winter impossible.

The industry doesn't ship by barge any longer, but the system remains.

Because books were originally on paper, there's a limited range to their size and length. There are few 12 page books, and none that are 4,000 pages long. The physics of the medium help determine the prices, advances, and variety as well.

The industry finds half of its sales in digital formats now, but the system remains.

It costs quite a bit to publish a book, so there's a finite number of books published each year. It stayed at around 40,000 a year for generations.

Independent bookstores were big enough to carry most of the books that mattered to most people, but not nearly big enough to carry all the books. That meant that shelf space was paramount, and promotion drove many decisions.

In fact, the number of books published was exactly the right number to make it so that the typical store was precisely the right size.

A book that sold a lot of copies would be more promoted by the publisher and the bookstore because it was more profitable to focus on promoting the books that were hits. Compounding this, books that made the bestseller list were more likely to be read by others, because many people only read books that are bestsellers.

The system runs deep. Successful publishers were in a symbiotic relationship with successful bookstores, since they didn't have nearly enough money to market directly to readers. The culture was often changed by books because the sort of person with cultural influence was also the sort of person that read books.

There were resilient feedback loops at every step.

And then the system changed. Slowly, and then all at once.

A giant online bookstore that sold every single book, at the best price, with free delivery. Digital books that cost nothing to create, store, or ship. The death of the independent bookstore as a cultural and economic force. And the rise of countless alternatives to books, carrying ideas via short and long snippets of video, audio, or text, all instantly and all for free.

The number of books published each year in the US (by the major publishers) has increased by a factor of 10. The initial orders from bookstores for new books have dropped by at least that much.

The fine people in book publishing would like it to remain as it was, and could pretend for a while. But when the foundational underpinnings of a system disappear, the system changes.

The Erie Canal doesn't matter.

It's easiest to see a system when it stops functioning as it did.

197. MAY I SEE THE ORG CHART?

I didn't know enough to ask.

We were selling internet marketing in 1994, long before that was a thing. I was in a meeting with a VP at IBM, and it was clear that she understood what we were doing and liked it.

She asked me for my pad, grabbed her pen, and started to draw.

A minute later, she turned the pad around and showed me the org chart of her division.

As she described who had real power and who had apparent authority, she was filling in the chart and circling some of the names. She said, "This guy will take a meeting and completely waste your time. He's nice but no one cares about his opinion. On the other hand, if you can persuade this person, you're good to go..."

This was what the decision-making system in their marketing department looked like. She understood that there was no point in hiding it—if vendors didn't know how it worked, they'd simply waste everyone's time and energy.

Each person on the chart was there to do a job, each might have meant well, but the architecture of status, who had a budget and the guts to use it—these were the invisible forces that required a strategy to address.

198. THE AGENT OF CHANGE

Systems change. They are dynamic.

When an event occurs that stresses a system, the rules of the system change, as do the outputs.

In our lifetimes, one of the most significant agents of change has been technology.

Sixty years ago, the development of the transistor led to inexpensive pocket radios with an earpiece. As a result, for the first time teenagers could listen to the radio on their own, without using their parents' large expensive stereo. This shifted the consumption of music, led to the growth of a different sort of radio programming, and shifted the entire music industry. The launch of FM radio a few years later compounded this.

When Jeff and Mackenzie Bezos got in their car and drove from New York to Seattle, they knew that the internet would change many industries, and made a list of which one to begin with. Small changes (like a simple online store that sold books) led to a cascading series of ever-larger changes, transforming the status quo in how things are designed, manufactured, shipped and sold.

The container ship was an agent of change for the American furniture industry. A closely knit system of stores, lumber producers, designers and fabricators that was centered in North Carolina was transformed by a device that enabled new competitors from overseas to ship furniture to the US extremely cheaply. Each element of the system changed as a result.

YouTube was an agent of change for magicians. Not only were magic stores largely replaced by PenguinMagic.com, which could demonstrate any trick at any time, but magicians could now develop an online following in the millions—at the same time that any performance would be dissected and revealed over time. The act of learning, performing, connecting, and making a living were all transformed by changing something live and intimate into a digital performance.

Solar lanterns are an agent of change for the ecosystem of small villages in India and other largely rural countries. With light at night, learning and family life changes. With the ability to charge a cell phone, the price received for farmed goods is revealed, and access to tools and information increases. And with the increase in earnings this leads to, larger power systems can be purchased, new tools can be powered, and the very nature of daily life is transformed.

199. LOOKING FOR THE AGENT OF CHANGE

The agent of change often takes the form of:

- Communications
- Competition
- Community action and regulation
- The means of production and access to capital
- Easing or creation of constraints
- Cultural shifts

When the foundation that a system is built on shifts, the system will fight back, but widespread and significant changes in these underpinnings often lead to permanent changes (and opportunities for those that see them coming).

One reason that venture capitalists were so excited about the dawn of the commercial internet (and then again with artificial intelligence) is that it checked all six of these boxes at once.

Here are some change agents through the ages:

- The car opened the door for fast food restaurants.

- Craigslist destroyed the business model for many newspapers. Spinoffs created a new communications layer that dramatically decreased public prostitution.

- MTV enabled the rise of rap music by decreasing the power of local radio stations.

- Home improvement TV shows led to the popularity of the Mc-Mansion.

- Birth control transformed the workforce and led to the rise of convenience foods.

- 800 numbers and the credit card transformed any organization that dealt with customers.

- The smart phone surfaced information about travelers and drivers, enabling Uber to transform the taxi industry.

- Casual Friday started a cascade that led to a significant shift in the creation and sale of the clothes we wear every day.

- The elevator permitted real estate developers to create skyscrapers and remade the idea of downtown, the same way that work from home is undoing much of that density.

- Junk bonds, hedge funds, and other financial instruments led to the rise and fall of big box stores, supermarket chains, and other leveraged businesses.

- AI is transforming farming.

- The coming reset in the price of carbon will transform just about everything.

The two most chosen jobs in the United States are truck driver and real estate broker.

Both are part of very well-established systems, and technology and the law are turning those systems upside down.

The first change agent for truck drivers is data—shippers now have far more knowledge of the supply chain and the conditions of transport.

Add to this self-driving long-haul trucks and the entire industry is transformed.

And the system of real estate has been upended by a combination of data transparency (Zillow, etc.) and recent settlements that upend the traditional monopoly that brokers had on fees.

These are either threats or opportunities. The smart strategy is to bet on change. How will the new system create opportunities for people brave enough to take them?

200. THE TELEGRAPH AND THE SKYSCRAPER

In order for cities to develop sufficient density, they needed skyscrapers. Before high-rise office buildings, all we had were sprawling villages.

In order to have skyscrapers, we needed the elevator to be invented.

But the elevator was insufficient. In the era of the telegraph, offices couldn't possibly be many stories tall—the number of messengers running in and out with telegrams would choke any means of getting up to the higher floors.

It was only the invention of the telephone that permitted knowledge workers to have an office in a skyscraper. Alexander Graham Bell changed real estate.

If you look for a change agent, you can find one.

201. CHEESE BULLIES

Oliver Zahn runs an insurgent tech company named Climax that uses science to make breathtakingly good cheese using only plants. It works with chefs to produce products that are delicious without apology.

Mateo Kehler had this to say about Climax, "One could make the argument that this is like a fraudulent cheese." Kehler continued, "As a cheesemaker, it's a fraud. It looks like a cheese. It might taste like a cheese. But it's not. It's not connected to our historical understanding of what cheeses are."

This is the system fighting back. Other unnamed, powerful folks in the cheese industry worked behind the scenes to rescind Climax's win in the Good Foods awards. These awards carry prestige and status in the food industry, and Climax's blue cheese was set to win (beating out cheeses made from cows.)

Why would hardworking, caring folks get so upset about a new kind of cheese?

Status and affiliation. Kehler isn't in the cow business. He's in the business of taking a commodity raw material and turning it into a high-value food item. It shouldn't matter to him whether the raw material is from a cow, a chickpea, or a nut.

But it does.

This is similar to the way the book industry acts—as if it's in the cutting-down-trees business instead of the enterprise of bringing new ideas to people who want to pay for them.

Or why, in 1960, Penn Central railroad missed their chance to build a successful airline. Trains had been the dominant form of long-haul travel for a century, but the airplane was now arriving as a faster, higher-status form of connection and transport.

Like Western Union before it, dominant companies like Penn Central could have made the move to the new wave. But, as Ted Levitt helped us understand in *Marketing Myopia*, they thought they were in the business of trains, not transportation.

They defended the system they were familiar with instead of building a system for the future.

In all of these cases, the bullies aren't being irrational. They're simply having trouble expressing what they actually want. They mistakenly believe that what they do is more important than why they do it.

They seek status, affiliation, and freedom from fear.

The status that comes from expertise and success.

The affiliation that comes from a place in an industry, one that's been stable for a century or more.

The desire to avoid the fear of the unknown and the need to protect the status quo.

After the dust settles down, the cheese bullies always look small-minded and stuck. But in the moment, it's easy to use power and authority if it helps you believe you can avoid a shaky foundation in the future.

The irony is that the very status and affiliation that allow them to bully insurgents could also be powerful tools to help them invent the future instead.

202. A BRIEF HISTORY OF JAYWALKING

Who gets the right of way and the benefit of the doubt? For millennia, the answer was easy: humans on foot.

The move to make cars superior to pedestrians began in 1913. The first recorded jaywalker shamer—"jay" was an insult, a term for a rube, a hick, someone from the country—was none other than Santa Claus. An actor stood in front of a department store in Syracuse and harangued pedestrians to get out of the way and let cars pass.

Within a decade, the car industry was coming together to change the culture in cities. When citizens in the city of Cincinnati proposed a bill that would limit the top speed of cars within the city limits, local businesses banned together to defeat it.

For the first time in millennia, the hierarchy of right of way was changing. Collisions that were described as grisly attacks on pedestrians by selfish drivers were now being characterized as errors by the victims.

Cars offered businesses access to well-off customers. They sped up transport and communication. Businesses didn't want to be left out. The car was more profitable for them.

A "safety committee" in Detroit offered a free service to lazy journalists. They could submit the details of a traffic collision and the staff of the committee would rewrite it to put the blame on the pedestrian.

Organizations even hired Boy Scouts to hand out postcards explaining the "safe" way to cross the street.

In less than a decade after Santa Claus led the way, there were anti-jaywalking laws in many cities, and the culture had changed.

Cars offered power, status, convenience, and network effects. Pedestrians never had a chance.

203. WHAT WILL I TELL THE OTHERS?

That's the second question. The first question is, "Why will I tell the others?"

How will the network you're building benefit me? Will it increase my status, enhance my social affiliation, or decrease my fear?

The network effect powers us through this. It gives us a reason.

And then the second question: Have we made it easy for you to tell the others?

Plenty of project creators would like their project to scale. They see an advantage in the efficiencies and leverage that comes from more people being connected. Uber, for example, needs scale with respect to riders in order to recruit drivers (and vice versa). Without scale it fails.

This is not the network effect.

The network effect is empathic—it asks, "Why would someone invite a friend into this network?" They're not going to do it because it makes your project work better.

The fax machine created a network effect. You can't send a fax to yourself (you'd get a busy signal). Instead, your fax machine works better if you have colleagues you can fax. So you recruit them.

The network effect offers the person spreading the idea a benefit—social standing, perhaps, but often something more practical. If Sue gets Bob in sync with her tools or her ideas, her day gets better. It not only gives them a reason to spread the idea, but gives them something to say when they do so.

When we offer utility, status, or affiliation to our users, they're more likely to use the systems leverage they have to find us more users.

204. WHO SAYS YES?

Working in the system means we need each person to say "yes." Someone says yes because it's their job to do so. They say yes because it gives them status, or pleases their boss.

On the other hand, when we're working to change the system, we will encounter individuals who are rewarded for saying "no" to our work.

That's how the status quo is maintained—the system sticks around because it's designed to stick around, and it's good at it.

But each individual in the system has mixed incentives. When the pressures on an individual are great enough, when the stories, timing, and culture all align, that individual may end up making a new decision based on new information.

Working on the system means turning someone who wants to say no into someone who says yes. Doing this with persistence over time cascades a single shift into several shifts. It's a chance to create new standards and a different culture.

205. IF YOU WANT TO USE THE SYSTEM

...you'll need to see it.

Consider the book industry analogy. From 1900 to 2015, you could change the culture with a book. Find an agent, which sends a signal to the publisher you need. The publisher might respond to a proposal for a book which matches the genre they publish in. They work with bookstores, media, other authors, organize a tour, produce galley copies and more to ensure that the stores sell 10,000 copies in the first week. *The New York Times*, part of this system, features the book on the bestseller list. That sends a signal to the next circle of buyers, and after that, it's left to the ideas in the book to be strong enough for readers to tell other readers.

Now, in the new world of ideas, very few of these steps make any rational sense. A book like *Fourth Wing* by Rebecca Yarros has more than 100,000 reviews on Amazon. It was a nationwide bestseller, and yet the author used few of the pieces of the original bookselling system to achieve this success.

To move an idea outside of a book transforms it even more. It's not unusual for a TikTok video of an idea to reach 1,000 times as many people as a book might.

The forces on the system exist long before the system itself changes.

206. THE PERSON IN FRONT OF YOU IS PART OF A SYSTEM

But they aren't the system.

No one makes decisions for the system. The invisible hand has no owner. Not even the president/founder/COO/monarch has complete control over the system.

Instead, each person in the system imagines what actions are likely to lead to the most useful responses. Useful for them. Useful today.

A few members of the system have enough oversight to want to hear how a new decision will impact the system as a whole. But even for these folks, no matter how well-meaning, the decision is driven by how the system will react.

We make two errors, again and again:

- When pitching an idea, we imagine that the person we're talking to cares primarily about the entire system, about what it should want. They don't. They're not even aware of the entire system. They're simply thinking about their boss, or their urgent needs, or nothing much at all.

- And when considering a change, we often revert to thinking about our limited agency and the person right in front of us, instead of probing for what might make the system itself pivot and shift.

207. SOME OF THE WAYS THAT SYSTEMS OPERATE

People within a system make voluntary choices about how they treat others who seek to engage with their system.

Successful people within the system are aware of their status compared to others in the system, and also seek affiliation with their peers.

People have scarce time and resources, and usually seek to reduce risk.

The default choice is to do what they've done before.

Sometimes, people involved in a system seek out performance metrics as a way to maintain status.

Often, people find that affiliating with those that have earned status in the community gives them status as well.

Invisible systems are often more powerful, because the participants in the system imagine the rules instead of reading them with an eye toward bending them.

Persistent systems work to maintain the status quo.

One way a system becomes persistent is by withholding short-term benefits to those that threaten the status quo.

Another way is by punishing heretics in the long-term.

It might seem that a person supporting a system "isn't doing their job." But the system demands support, and that might actually be their job.

One of the most powerful agents of change is a technology or shift that gives some users of the system more choices, especially if those choices alter the status dynamics.

An elegant strategy doesn't decry these tendencies. It simply adjusts to them. By giving the nodes what they want, it produces value while also changing the standards, information flow, and outputs.

208. TYPES OF ELEGANT STRATEGIES

Low cost and low price: This is the most common one to chase, but rarely achieved. Walmart didn't reinvent retail simply by lowering their prices. They also lowered their costs, and they did it so persistently and consistently that no one could catch up for decades, even when the playbook was obvious.

Low cost doesn't simply mean trying harder. It's a systemic advantage you have built into your organization, one that gets better as you scale.

Bringing things over in container ships allowed Walmart to sell things for less than their competition could even buy them. As they grew and their volume went up, they were able to use warehouse logistics to sell items less than thirty days after they received them—meaning that not only could they buy things for less, but they were paying their suppliers *after* they had sold the product, essentially getting free working capital as they grew.

Low cost is easy to claim but hard to do. Many organizations claim that this is what they do, but they end up with only the low-price part. If you don't have a substantial process advantage, low prices are almost impossible to maintain.

It's a race to the bottom and you might win. Cut enough corners and there's nothing left. And resilience disappears.

Maintaining the upper end of luxury: Some of the most valuable brands in the world are doing precisely the opposite. Hermès and LVMH relentlessly raise the price of everything they sell, and have built marketing and production systems to ensure that they remain the gold standard for shoppers who insist on paying more. While the retailers at these institutions are tempted every day to lower their prices to gain market share, resisting this impulse for centuries is at the heart of their model.

The network effect: If you offer a service or a product that works better when my friends use it, I'm likely to tell my friends. This isn't an afterthought or a marketing gimmick— it's at the heart of product design and user experience. People don't share because they like you. They share because it helps them achieve their objectives.

Alcoholics Anonymous isn't anonymous, and you can't do it by yourself. That's the point.

Expertise and status: The hallmark of an elegant strategy is that the more you use it, the better it works. Harvard has been around since before Galileo Galilei was killed, and their head start compounds with each generation.

Their status attracts professors seeking status, which attracts students, and funders, and scholarly journals, and discussion, and jobs, all creating a loop that's hard to break.

When Chris Anderson bought TED more than 20 years ago, it was a tiny conference with 300 attendees annually. He poured accelerant on the strategy by posting the recorded talks online, which attracted viewers, which made giving a talk more attractive, until, more than a billion views later, it's seen as an institution. The fact that it has a built-in network effect made the model even more powerful.

Affiliation: The desire to fit in is the fuel for the status quo in fashion, regardless of whether it's clothing, language, or cultural discourse.

The most profitable brands overinvest in finding and confirming affiliation among their customers. People have a long history of trading money for belonging.

Committing to a technology or cultural curve: Moore's Law isn't just a good idea, it actually is the law. For the last 60 years, the costs of computer chips keeps going down while their power goes up. If cars had the same yield curve as computer chips, you could buy a Porsche today for $50. There are similar curves in our culture, including an increase in diversity in background, gender, and race. There are relentless curves in climate, artificial intelligence, and digital connection as well.

Is tomorrow going to be more in your favor than today was? Elegant strategies often go with the current, not against it.

The coyote: Lewis Hyde describes this role as the trickster. In Indigenous traditions, the coyote is the agent of change, the provocateur, the one who finds a crack in the system and exploits it.

It's exhausting to do this on a regular basis, but it's a role that systems depend on. Andy Warhol was a coyote, and so is the MSCHF website. Always probing, provoking, and inventing, the coyote brings change to the system, often at a personal cost.

Doing the work of a coyote isn't predictable and it's difficult to scale. Many coyote organizations end up purchased by organizations that dominate the industry—either to absorb the magic they bring or to silence them.

When an insurgent begins to become a standard bearer, it's almost impossible to maintain the coyote role. David Letterman, Miles Davis, and even the Who became the establishment that they railed against.

The status quo: Successful systems fight to maintain the status quo in which they are successful. Organizations and individuals that offer to help in this fight are always in high demand.

When the research and advisory company Gartner highlighted the potential risks of the Y2K problem 20 years ago, they had plenty of demand for their advice from large corporations. Potential risk remediation is a complicated way to say, "everything will be okay (if you listen to us)."

The problem with this approach is that sooner or later, the status quo falls when confronted by a change agent. You probably don't want to be Sears or Walden Books or Western Union. But it always happens if we wait long enough.

Subscriptions and convenience: A variation of maintaining the status quo, organizations that sell subscriptions are selling peace of mind and convenience.

When Lester Wunderman moved to rural France, he discovered one cold night that the oil heating truck only came if you called them. He persuaded one company to sell him an ongoing subscription instead.

Consumers realize that they might pay more by not shopping around each time, but they happily sign up because not running out is worth more than saving a few dollars.

Reinvesting the head start: As we've seen, systems amplify head starts. An organization that reinvests more than its peers will have better processes, more reliable outputs, and unattainable technology. The result is that it will enhance their head start, with changes in the system or the technology regularly producing more of a lead.

"No one ever got fired for buying IBM" was true for 40 years. It wasn't because they had the best tech for any given problem (they rarely did). It was because they created so much reassurance, cultural advantage, and convenience that it was easier to say "yes" than to risk shopping around.

Singularly focused market disruption: Unlike the coyote, the organization that finds one leverage point to shift a system is able to eventually become the agent of change. The system survives, of course, but it's transformed by the change and eventually takes it for granted, as if it's always been this way.

That's certainly the effect of the iPhone, but it's also true for something as apparently minor as the U.S. News College Rankings, or the creation of the shipping container.

FedEx bet everything that they'd be able to transform the system with a centralized, nationwide small package delivery business. There was no half-success possible here. Either the dynamic of speedy business shipments became the standard for law firms and corporations, or they would fail.

209. BRINGING CHANGE TO A SYSTEM

Several things determine how an existing system will respond to a change agent.

- Does adapting to the change require a different set of metrics, rewards, and approaches?

- Does the change lead to a significant change in the dominant status structure—one that those in power will seek to stop?

- Does the change rhyme with previous changes, and does the system have a history of accepting and working with these sorts of changes?

- Is the problem or insight the agent of change brings persistent and permanent, or is it transient or simply urgent?

- Do other systems benefit from the change in a way that will threaten the power of this system?

- Does the change align with the unstated values and beliefs of the system?

- Is the change perceived as a threat to individual roles, skills, or job security of the nodes that have power?

- Do nodes in the system believe they have the necessary resources and capabilities to implement the change?

- Will competitive pressures force the system to adopt the change?

We can see examples of this analysis in systems large and small, new and old.

When the technology of the telephone arrived, the existing players in the telegraph communications system didn't respond with enthusiasm. The center of the network, Western Union, turned down a chance to buy the Bell technology.

The companies and individuals that sent and received and profited from telegraphy weren't eager to switch, and imagined that the telephone was simply a novelty for wealthy urban dwellers.

IBM and Digital were giant computer companies that were certain that the market for the personal computer was less than 20,000 units. They both waited a very long time before acknowledging the shift.

The same thing happened when cable TV began to gain in popularity. While CBS helped start ESPN, most of the major players in the TV system, including the hardware companies, talent agencies, local stations, and actors ignored the new medium, giving upstarts like Ted Turner plenty of room to innovate.

The legal system, on the other hand, was an early user of online databases, because it amplified the power of lawyers while decreasing the influence of lower-status clerks and librarians. In addition, the lawyers who embraced it won more cases, so the competitive pressure was real.

This analysis isn't reserved for large-scale systems. The same insight can be brought to a small profession, like gastroenterologists (who ignored insights about the causes of ulcers), or to the social services agencies in a small town (in how they responded to a new threat like Fentanyl overdoses).

210. LUCK DOESN'T EVEN OUT IN THE LONG RUN

Philosopher Dan Dennett was wrong. He claimed that luck evens out. Alas, if you start a metaphorical marathon behind the leaders, you're unlikely to catch up through luck. In the words of Neil Levy, "We cannot undo the effects of luck with more luck."

Systems contain feedback loops, and the loops often reward an early lead. It's more productive to go faster now than it is to go faster later.

When a six-year-old kid beats the other kids at tennis, that kid is more likely to be encouraged to play more, or to get a coach, and pretty soon, they're much better at tennis than the others. That leads to more coaches and more tournaments.

When a musical group has a single that gets some buzz on Spotify, they're more likely to be able to find a producer or even a label.

When a candidate polls well early in a race, they're more likely to get donations, attract consultants, run ads and not be encouraged to drop out.

There are scarcity-based competitions in our culture that reward early success. Acknowledging this (however unfair or suboptimal it is as a sorting mechanism) informs how we think about our strategy.

We can decide to play in a system where our head start gives us a natural advantage. Or we can acknowledge that the feedback loops in the system are probably not going to help us at first, and we can work to find the support and coaching we need to overcome this. Scaffolding is hard to find and priceless.

There are often ways forward if we're willing to look for them.

211. LEVERAGE AND THE EXAGGERATION OF STRATEGIES

Leverage in business works like this: Something is working, and you borrow some money to help it work louder, faster, or at more scale.

You have a machine that improves efficiency. Borrow some money and buy a second machine. Now you have even *more* efficiency.

Each strategy can be amplified with investment.

So what's the problem?

Your competition is borrowing money too with the same idea you have—with this investment, we'll be able to scale our strategy.

Small leads are amplified because leaders can borrow more money. But when there are investors to pay back, nuance goes out the window. Employees get squeezed, and then customers do.

It's hard to hold back and bring a sensible approach to scale because your competitors are in a race to outdo you.

This leads to Schumpeter's creative destruction. *Any strategy, scaled big enough, cannot be sustained, and it will be replaced by a new set of conditions, players, and rules.*

In other words: Every successful organization will fail unless it becomes something different before it does.

212. INTENT AND SIDE EFFECTS

When a system is created, the intent is usually a good one.

The pioneers of the internet weren't trying to build a platform for trolls and misogynists. The creators of packaged foods weren't hoping to increase obesity, diabetes, and heart attacks.

But side effects often occur.

Side effects are merely effects. The system produces them, often with the same reliable regularity as the desired effects. If we can't accept the side effects, then we can't accept the system.

A strategy cannot ignore the side effects. Because side effects are part of the system, the same way that a shadow is part of the sunshine.

213. TURBULENCE AND SYSTEMS TRANSFORMATION

A system in a steady state is exactly that—steady. While there are always ripples of change at various nodes in the system, the overall situation remains fairly predictable.

The volunteer fire department, funeral traditions, and boarding schools are all relatively unchanged after a century or more.

But sometimes a change agent finds the leverage for the system to be transformed. The internet is one of those agents. So is the smart phone.

But climate change also acts as an agent of change, as does the rising power of women and overlooked social castes.

When an entrenched system encounters a new technology or cultural shift that threatens the status quo, it may ignore it, fight it, or seek to live with it. But sometimes, the system itself is transformed.

When that happens, it's accompanied by turbulence. Turbulence is unexpected, chaotic, and usually temporary.

In moments of turbulence, new ideas and new organizations can gain traction and further the transformation. It's easy to imagine that the turbulence will last forever, but it rarely does.

The Hollywood system lasted a century, until the change agent of online media and the long tail turned it upside down. This permitted a new sort of celebrity to arise (what a sad name "influencer" is) as well as a shift in where our culture looked for cues and inspiration.

214. GATEKEEPERS

The goal of an editor is to keep things normal.

They choose to publish the sorts of work their readers are used to and ready for. They seek out ideas that match or rhyme with the ones that came before.

For centuries, influential science journals have rejected important new ideas. Here are a few:

Plate Tectonics: It took decades before geologists accepted this theory.

Helicobacter pylori **and Ulcers:** In 1982, Australian physicians Barry Marshall and Robin Warren proposed that the bacterium *Helicobacter pylori* was responsible for causing most peptic ulcers, challenging the prevailing belief that ulcers were caused by stress and lifestyle factors. Decades years later they won the Nobel prize.

The Alvarez Hypothesis: In 1980, father-and-son team Luis and Walter Alvarez proposed that a massive asteroid impact led to the extinction of the dinosaurs. Decades later, it was finally widely accepted.

One reason for the rejections is that each innovation was from an outsider. An outsider using different approaches or crossing traditional boundaries. Another is that the new idea threatens the status quo without sufficient support (ironically, that support mostly comes from appearing in a journal).

The gatekeeper isn't there to help the creator get attention. They exist to give the system warmth and reassurance. Sometimes, the job of a gatekeeper is to keep the gate closed.

The very same gatekeeping happened with network TV executives, with the A&R person at Decca who rejected the Beatles, and with mass merchants who refuse to carry items that go on to big success online.

How do new ideas get past the gatekeeper who seeks to maintain the status quo?

In the case of scientific papers, it often happens at conferences. Talks plus pre-print papers handed out. A few other scientists are converted and they spread the word. This is how chaos theory came to be accepted.

In music, FM radio broke the logjam. New gatekeepers led to significant upstream changes to the system.

Twenty years later, mix tapes, local DJs, and ultimately MTV allowed rap to spread without any help at all from traditional music gatekeepers.

And TikTok and YouTube have transformed which cultural ideas spread by video.

Without traditional gatekeepers, the cycle speeds up.

215. KINDS OF TENSION

A system in a steady state is organized to keep tension as low as possible. Maintenance of the status quo offers reassurance and freedom from fear.

Change offered or demanded creates tension in the system.

If there were no tension, everyone would either instantly switch to the new paradigm or ignore what's on offer. It's that in-between state—the state of wanting and fearing at the same time—that almost all of us live in.

Part of the empathy of creating positive change is that we can see the desires of those we serve, and also juxtapose that with the fears that change will cause. *We are causing fear.*

We get to choose to create that tension, and we can find a strategy that supports the tension that gives us a chance to move our project forward. Here are some of the options:

As little tension as possible: The default is to offer something that's more convenient, cheaper, and verified. In essence, hoping our work will slip in without much of a ripple. This is more for less. It's not only less money, it's easier too.

This turns out to be a special case. It's special because it's easy to hope for and very difficult to accomplish. The freelancer who says, "You can pick anyone, and I'm anyone," has a rough go of it.

Important work looks past the goal of no tension and instead seeks out and balances the varieties of fear that humans manage to invent. These fears often work in conflict with one another—we cause one kind of problem but promise to reduce another kind. Someone will run from one fear and toward another one.

Our project relieves the tension once it's adopted by those in our community. There's a hump, and on the other side, there is better.

The fear of missing the new thing: Early adopters seek novelty. If you create an innovation, you've built an attractor for people who seek innovation.

The fear of being left behind: When a system begins to adopt a new idea, particularly one that amplifies a head start, others will follow because they can feel the tension that comes with waiting.

The fear of being left out: This isn't quite the same as being left behind. This is the "everyone else is already doing this" tension of group dynamics.

The generosity of the network effect: When a colleague or friend asks you to join as a favor to them, there's tension about not granting this request.

The fear of being seen as a fraud: Surprisingly common, rarely talked about, it usually helps us avoid shortcuts and hustles, but it also holds us back from embracing bravery.

What will I tell my boss? Even nodes that aren't eager to explore new frontiers are aware that their organization might want them to do so.

And there are more:
The fear of failing, and its surprising cousin, the fear of succeeding.
The fear of responsibility.
The fear of speaking out or speaking up.
The fear of being judged.
The fear of being out of sync.
The fear of the new or the unfamiliar.
The fear of strangers.
The fear of insufficiency.
The fear of the end.
And the reason it's so difficult to talk about this: **the fear of fear.**

216. "WHAT WILL I TELL THE OTHERS?"

That's at the heart of engaging with a node in the system. Someone in a system can't do something brave and powerful and new without telling their boss and their peers.

If someone is going to make an unusual hiring decision, change a policy, or even buy from a new supplier, they're exposing themselves to risk—a risk that the system amplifies, because the system's stability is based on maintaining the status quo.

The successful intervention pre-writes the story. It eliminates the unstated objection before it becomes a factor.

It's a pattern match. The thing we already agreed is important… this helps us get that thing. In fact, to stall or debate is to undermine our commitment to the thing we said mattered.

No single node changes an entire system. We're seeking systems within systems, cadres of mutual support. Smaller groups that seek to connect and gain status with each other, with new groups coming aboard as the culture changes.

217. TWO TESLA PARABLES: LUDICROUS AND THE CLOWN CAR

The Model S is a case study of the useful application of tension.

When it first launched, the position was, "All of the things you like about a top-of-the-line Mercedes, but it will make you look like you're smarter than your friends."

It became the bestselling luxury car in California for this reason. The early adopters adopted, and then plenty of luxury car buyers followed, because they didn't want to fall behind or look like technophobes.

It's worth noting that the number one thing that prompted conversations in parking lots (according to a Tesla insider) was the retracting door handles. People would walk over to a new Tesla and ask—not about the value of electric cars, or the shift they represented—about the cool door handles.

Which led to the invitation to hop in and go for a spin. "Ludicrous mode" wasn't particularly functional, but great fun to talk about. When activated, the car would accelerate 50% faster than any traditional car could. It would silently scream from 0 to 60 in a few seconds, leading the passengers to actually scream.

The tension the car caused demanded to be talked about, and for many drivers, it led to enough discomfort with the status quo that they switched.

A few years later, Tesla announced the Cybertruck.

Years into the life of the company, Tesla had earned the right to cross the chasm and show up for a mass market. Alas, they missed their chance. Artlessly designed, the truck caused little of the tension for forward motion that the Model S created.

Pickup trucks are the best-selling vehicles in the US, and Tesla was in a perfect spot to dominate the segment of the market that was able and willing to purchase an expensive electric alternative. But pickup truck drivers are more likely to buy something proven, conservative, and low key, because that's what their truck is for. The truck is not only a signifier of wealth or luxury, it's a signifier of utility—even, and especially, for people who don't need the utility.

Instead of making it easy for the buyer to talk about how "normal" and "useful" it was (key factors in buying a truck), Tesla focused on bulletproof windows (that failed in the demo) and Mad Max features that shouted at anyone who drove by. The only story the truck let people tell was, "I'm a fanboy."

As a result, there were plenty of preorders from fans, and not much in the way of ongoing support from anyone else. Resale value is down by 50%.

The smallest viable audience is most useful, but only when serving them is a seed that grows into a larger segment of the market, causing the change you seek.

218. COMPETITIVE ADVANTAGE

Most discussions of strategy begin and end with an understanding of competitive advantage.

Competitive advantage is often based on the flawed assumption that all other things are equal and that every day, people in the marketplace are making a new rational decision among similar options.

If there are two avocados at the market and one is riper, larger, and less blemished, of course someone is going to pick that one. If a farmer has found a varietal and a supply chain that lets her regularly deliver a better avocado, she'll gain in market share.

And it's possible to buy your way into a short-term competitive advantage. You can deliver more for less, take less margin, lose a bit of money, and try much harder than is consistently feasible. But a short-term competitive advantage isn't helpful unless it leads to a systemic change you can sustain.

There are investments we can make to cause a change over time. Through design, productivity investments, and storytelling, we can find a long-term competitive advantage.

Traditionally, organizations have focused on a few pillars to win in the marketplace:

- Reliable quality through process innovation

- Better price

- Intellectual property

- Persistent positioning advantage

- Customer service

- Distribution lock-in

- Product innovation

- Specialization

- Partnerships

You've heard of all of these before. Build a better mousetrap, create a moat around your brand, invest in machines and processes that are more efficient, and partner in ways that box out the competition.

They all contribute to the long-lasting goal of competitive advantage: "This is the one the system wants."

If it's what the system wants, you can charge a fair price. It has a network effect built-in, so substitutes are suspect and have less utility. It provides you with enough margin and momentum that you can continue to reinvest to make sure the system keeps wanting it. It's a feedback loop you can maintain.

219. METCALFE'S LAW IS WAITING FOR YOU

Trust leads to trust. Influence creates influence. The network effect is the dynamic of our time, and most of us don't even notice it.

The value of a network goes up exponentially as more people engage with it.

People don't engage with your network because it's good for you. They do it because it's good for them. The network effect challenges system architects to create assets that provide value for users that increase when they invite their colleagues to join in.

This is one reason why luck doesn't even out. A smart strategy creates the conditions for a network effect, and the resulting exponential growth compounds into value—value for the creator of the network, but also value for the people who are part of it.

Shawn Coyne explained that the author's job is to sell the first 10,000 copies of a book, and then it's the book's job to sell the rest.

The "book" is the work, the thing we create. It's the artifact that people in the network use to recruit other people to the network. Not because they like the work, but because the work (when shared) will help them achieve their goals.

It doesn't have to be a book. It's the online community or the pizza parlor. It's the movement for a sustainable future or the performance at a jazz club that the pianist wants to sell out.

The network effect powers every cultural change or business project.

220. THE FIRST RULE...

It's not only the fax machine, or Fight Club, or Alcoholics Anonymous. The network effect powers any system that deserves it.

This isn't a competition of effort or obvious performance metrics. The work doesn't get the network effect it deserves based on how much you insist on people joining you. Instead, networks catch on because the network being built is attractive, sticky, and persistent. Does it work better for me if my friends join in?

Networks create value for those who choose to join them, and part of that value comes from the status and affiliation bump that evangelists of the system receive.

People only invite others to join a network if they benefit from doing so.

If you don't begin with a network effect as a significant benefit for users, it's almost impossible to build it in later.

221. DO VS. WANT

What people do might not be aligned with what they want.

We all have bad habits, and that's without community or peer pressure to amplify them. Every organization has bad habits, and every system filled with people ends up doing things that don't match their stated principles and objectives.

Did the electoral system in the United States want the Vietnam war? Do aluminum baseball bat companies want little league players to be injured or die from their product? Did the team at Pepsi really want people to get diabetes from their optimized marketing maneuvers?

Probably not.

We can pivot the system when we help people do things that more effectively get them what they wanted all along.

We're not trying to tell them that what they want is wrong. That's a hard sell, and we probably don't have enough leverage to pull it off.

Instead, we're working to create the conditions for people to choose to do useful things while seeking what they've always wanted.

And what they want is status and affiliation. Some combination of joy, honor, and achievement. A place to be safe and a way to excel.

222. EXCHANGING THE SYSTEM IS TEMPTING

But unlikely. Revolutions cause trauma. It's possible to abruptly change a system—whether it's the economic structure of Russia turning into the USSR, or the dynamics of a failing public school replacing all the metrics and behaviors with urgency.

It's not recommended.

Culture defeats tactics, every time, and culture is the most resilient component of a system.

Often we have the opportunity to do judo instead of surgery. To embrace the goals and momentum of the system and direct it in a better direction.

We don't change the system as much as we change the outputs the system creates.

223. REVOLUTIONS ARE RARE

Change almost always involves a pivot. The change agent isn't changing what the nodes in the system want—they're changing how they get it.

DeBeers didn't change the way the patriarchy and those with wealth used weddings as a signifier of status and affiliation. Instead, they pivoted the system by making up a story about diamonds and celebrity and pride and longevity and status.

No one actually wants a diamond. They want the story it allows them to tell.

The folks at big industrial enterprises don't actually want to destroy the ecosystem. What they want is stability, status, and to please their boss. The pollution is simply a by-product.

When we tell a different story about how to achieve the wants they already have, behaviors shift.

Not via a revolution, but through a strategy and a story.

The car companies fought seat belts. They fought mandatory airbags. And they fought making the steering column safer.

Of course, it's not that the industry wanted people to die in horrible crashes. When that happens, they lose a customer. What they wanted was status, stability, and profits.

And then, in the face of coordinated community action, they discovered that they would have more stability and make more of a profit if they embraced the race for safety instead of fighting it.

224. THE GAME BELONGS TO THE CHILDREN WHO PLAY IT

The writer Simon Harling wants us to pay attention to the order in which things unfold. The unstated priorities that are baked into the system cause us to alter how we approach it and the work we do.

His blueprint for child sports begins with a vision for a different kind of system:

- Development > Competition.

- I don't care who wins.

- I do care that my children compete for and with each other.

- I don't care about the better players getting more game time.

- I do care that each child gets the same amount of playing time.

- I don't care that my best players play out of position.

- I do care that all my players play in every position on the pitch.

There are few soccer leagues that are built on these precepts, because most soccer parents are engaged in a different set of priorities.

Typical soccer parents seem to believe that soccer offers more fun, status, and excitement if their team wins. Winning requires a skills hierarchy, cutting players that don't perform, and finding an edge that can lead to a victory, even if it costs the players in the short run.

These parents create the conditions for kids to fear being teased for poor performance, and to extend themselves for whatever it takes to win. They act as though there's a trophy shortage, and they pursue easily measured metrics.

They're not bad parents or coaches—they're simply in a different system.

The existing system is resilient. It's easy to promote the idea of winning, to motivate kids and parents with points and pride and trophies. It's easier to get the community at large excited with the status that comes from a winning team.

The critical choice in building a blueprint for a different sort of league is to simply walk away from the other system. We can't easily shift someone's perspective, but we can work to find the people who want to go where we seek to go.

When that other league, the Harling league, begins to deliver benefits for the few kids and parents that are involved, the word will spread. A different sort of status and affiliation will accrue to the families that are early adopters, and those families may end up recruiting others.

It's easier to help someone find what they want than it is to change what they want.

225. THE TWO UNSEEN DESIRES

We're never on our own. We're surrounded by the forces created by cultural, environmental, and technical systems, and these systems have a lot to do with our ability to make change happen.

Classic economics argues that humans are rational decision-makers. When something cheaper or more functional comes along, we embrace it. When we can use our time or our resources to meet our goals, we do so.

And yet this almost never happens the way economists say it will. We almost never change the market or our communities the way we hope. This is largely due to unseen desires that are more powerful than we expect.

The unseen desires are worth naming: social adhesion and resistance to substitution.

Social adhesion is culture. People like us do things like this. The unspoken rules that cause us to do things that might not be easy or in our short-term interest. The vague (or pronounced) feelings we have when going against the grain.

And resistance to substitution is at the heart of every market we engage in. Why this and not that? What prevents a constant race for cheaper or more convenient? Shouldn't everything be a rational commodity?

Why stick when we can switch?

Social adhesion and resistance to substitution often work at cross purposes, creating an oscillating and unstable equilibrium between change and the status quo.

"Everyone else is doing it" meets "I don't want to go first."

Once you see the two desires, it becomes easier to identify and work with systems in your work or community.

Why does a 400-year-old institution like Harvard have a waiting list when similar classes are available online for free? We pay extra for name-brand vodka, even if we know it's made in the same factory as the generic stuff. And that yutz down the hall is secure in his job—a job we'd never hire him for if he applied today.

Or consider Prada's baseball cap, a $650 hat that offers no functional advantages over a $4 alternative—except that the social benefits of wearing one in some communities are large enough that for those purchasers, it's a bargain. There are countless substitutes, but none of them can offer precisely the same combination of status, affiliation, and belonging that this ridiculous item can offer to the right person.

Compare this to real estate brokers. It's not particularly difficult to become a real estate broker in the United States. There are millions of brokers. Whenever housing markets heat up, more brokers enter the market, substitutions are easy, and the average income per broker doesn't go up much. A willingness to switch changes market dynamics dramatically.

Back and forth we go—systems that support the status quo and change agents that encourage substitution and a new status quo.

Under these two forces are a handful of amplifiers—dynamics that keep systems powerful and stable.

Network effects are the enemy of substitution. If the popular choice works better because it's popular, people are not eager to switch. This explains why there's only one standard for fax machines and why it's better to have your profile on LinkedIn than on Friendster.

The **stickiness of leaders** (and the challenge for substitutes) runs deep. People don't want to "waste" a vote in an election, so they side with someone who is ahead in the polls. Popular tourist destinations remain popular because they're the place to go.

This is an example of a **feedback loop**. Feedback loops compound the small advantages of an early leader. Social cohesion demands that we be in sync with our peers, and the early signals of a lead often encourage us to pick that leader, expanding their head start.

Sunk costs then arrive to further lock-in an incumbent against possible substitutes. Humans often overvalue past decisions and then repeat them. We build this aversion into our social circles, rewarding people who stick with their traditions and previous decisions.

Status roles and **affiliation** are at the heart of social adhesion, and they're the driving force behind many of the individual decisions that add up to creating cultural standards.

Status roles are a measure of who's up and who's down. Power dynamics like these drive our choices, and comparing ourselves to others is a persistent human behavior.

Affiliation keeps us in orbit. Who's to our left and who's to our right? Do we fit in? Do we fit in enough?

When technology or external forces act as an **agent of change**, substitution is on offer. The invention of email, the electric car, or the gluten-free bakery offered every person a choice—who will benefit by going first and who will insist on going last (or never)?

226. THE THING ABOUT CHEAPER

Sometimes, people will pick the cheaper option.

Cheaper means less expensive, or less complicated, or more convenient.

In fact, people will pick the cheaper option any time that there isn't substitution aversion or a desire for social adhesion. All other things being equal, we always choose the cheaper option.

But things are almost never equal.

Things are affected by systemic forces. Social adhesion and substitution aversion are almost everywhere we look.

227. COMPOUNDING OUR TRIBAL INSTINCTS

The evolution of social adhesion isn't an accident. When we lived in groups of a hundred people, surrounded by an unfamiliar and often dangerous world, belonging to the group was a critical survival mechanism.

Add to this the instinct every species has to avoid the new, to fear mistakes, to avoid wasting time and energy, and you can see how substitution aversion can become easily ingrained. Seeking novelty is strange behavior, a symptom of becoming accustomed to wealth and safety.

As we developed the ability to make decisions, group dynamics pushed us to make a common series of errors when it came to rational consideration of our options.

Individuals with power (who desire to keep and amplify that power) benefit when we make decisions that benefit the existing social system, despite the cost to any individual in that system.

And while we're culturally primed to seek out something new (reruns are not part of must-see TV), there's a lot of social, commercial, and internal pressure to stick with what's safe.

Some examples:

Loss aversion: Losing feels worse than winning feels good, and it's easier to stand pat and protect what we have.

Confirmation bias: It's nice to feel like we made a good choice. The group encourages its members to look for external signs that existing choices were appropriate, and thus diminishes a desire to look for substitutes.

Tribalism: The strong loyalty to one's own tribe or social group (often leading to hostility or discrimination against those perceived as outsiders) can reinforce social adhesion within groups and make it harder for new ideas or practices to spread across group boundaries.

But most of all, in the last century, we took our instincts for social adherence and substitution aversion and built them into our culture.

The unspoken motto of Facebook is, "People are talking about you behind your back—do you want to hear what they're saying?"

The media puts us in a constant state of alert about new things that are happening (they even call it "breaking news").

Existing systems of status keep track of easily measured proxies and won't let them go: the Forbes 400 list of billionaires, the Oscars, or the desire that your wedding should be exactly like your friends' weddings (but a little nicer.)

Once the foundations for these systems are created, we build commerce around them, ensuring that they will stick around.

228. SUBSTITUTES AND THE RACE TO THE BOTTOM

Substitutes are efficient. They give us options, take power away from suppliers, and create resilience in the system.

But individual creators, workers, or producers benefit from working to avoid the substitution mindset. If you don't make a commodity, your work is more valued. "Accept no substitutes" is the opposite of "you can pick anyone and we're anyone." The useful strategy is to seek to avoid the race to the bottom.

There's enormous pressure to simply be a substitute, or to be substituted. To meet the spec, to answer the RFP and to fit in, all the way. Marketing and strategy work together to avoid this trap.

A brand is not a logo, and low price isn't a sustainable position for most organizations. The promise that a brand makes is valuable when users pay extra (in time or money) for that brand.

If you need to lower your prices to get repeat business, you don't have customer loyalty. And if you are regularly substituted, you don't have much of a brand.

If you make something that the system doesn't insist on, your market insulation disappears, and now you're competing on nothing but price or convenience.

It turns out that when a system has enough power to demand a commodity, it creates efficiency and resilience—and so the price of a ream of paper is vanishingly low, because if all paper is the same, we'll take the cheap one, thanks very much.

On the other hand, when a student is comparing an MIT degree to the benefit of taking the very same courses online for free, the bulk of value differentiation comes from what the system values—the degree, not the learning.

Are there substitutes for what you offer? Substitutes that the system accepts and admires?

The only honest answer is "yes". This means that the hard work is creating a product, an experience, and a story that's not worth finding a substitute for.

229. SEEKING THE INVISIBLE HAND

Systems worth examining have an element of the invisible to them.

The solar system has gravity. It works at a distance, unseen.

Market economics coordinate activities without a coordinator. A problem arises and organizations show up to solve it. Merchants build shops near each other. Prices stabilize, supply chains arrive. The people involved in creating and selling and buying a pencil don't coordinate their actions, and yet, the invisible hand brings the pencil we need to the person who needs it.

When bringing a project to the world, it pays to see the systems that will be pushing it forward or holding it back.

Here's what's worth investigating:

Who gains or loses in status from changes in the system?

Are there forms of communication and interoperability wired into the system?

What are the forces that oppose substitutions?

Are the individuals or nodes with the incentive and power to hold things back or push them forward? And are there other nodes that can work in opposition?

Are there behaviors that seem like superstitions based in history instead of reality?

Where are the feedback loops that amplify or diminish signals?

Most systems that are complex enough to be interesting are held together with tension. Individual nodes want different outcomes, but no one has enough power to insist, and so the system oscillates, with the invisible hand apparently moving from one edge to the other.

230. EXAMPLES OF SYSTEMS LIVING IN TENSION

The fine art world includes painters, collectors, investors, gallerists, forgers, auction houses, art shows, museum curators, cultural media, artisans, hangers-on and charlatans. They have different and sometimes conflicting agendas. Some fight to maintain the status quo, others push for change.

The system of industrialized medicine includes doctors, nurses, patients, families, lawyers, hospitals and their investors, pharmaceutical companies and their investors, scholarly journals, medical schools, insurance companies, government agencies, nursing homes, hospice workers, and social commentators.

One more: Schools involve parents, school boards, teachers, superintendents, boards of regents, students, placement offices, firms that are hiring, licensing boards, textbook publishers, the teacher's union, principals, and banks.

In each case, there are subgroups that have conflicting agendas, and even within subgroups there's tension.

But it's also true that the status quo rewards many of the players, particularly since they can't agree on anything to replace it. If they could, it would have changed already.

Beyond the conflicting agendas faced by complex systems, the entire system is often under tension as well. When technology changes, or public policy shifts, the system itself scrambles to find and maintain equilibrium.

We most easily see a system when the system bends under stress.

231. WHICH HAT?

It might be helpful to imagine that we can choose a persona for our project and our work. Each is appropriate in some circumstances—the trap lies in wearing one of these hats and then hoping for the result that comes from a different one.

Whether or not you actively choose a hat, you're wearing one. Or sometimes more than one, which is rarely a good look.

The insurgent: This project has enough speed, direction, and power to actually force the system to take notice. The status quo will fight back and sometimes succeed and survive. The Occupy movement was an insurgent that failed, while Chuck Berry and Elvis Presley succeeded.

The change agent: When the technology of production or communication fundamentally shifts, the existing system pretends it's not happening, tries to fight it, and ultimately fails or changes. Examples of this include the impact podcasts have had on traditional talk radio, or the inexorable shift in every element of our lives due to climate change.

The cobbler: This person does an important job in an existing system, and while not often paid fairly, toils away at their craft. Most freelancers fall into this category.

Fidei Defensor: The defender of the faith. Originally coined by Henry VIII, the "faith" being defended here is not necessarily religious but represents any set of traditional values, customs, or systems that are being challenged or questioned. It's a cheese bully, fighting against vegan cheese, or a music critic sneering about what's on the radio right now.

The innovator: Technology and insight are the most common and powerful ways to change a system. The innovation creates opportunities and threats, and the tension that builds around it forces existing players in the system to respond or react. Claude.ai and other LLM's are a current example. The work they do can become a change agent, but right now, the innovator is simply focused on solving an interesting problem.

The educator: Information is actually a measurable force of nature, as much as a rainstorm or a meteor. When information is shared and spread, the system shifts.

The maintainer and the optimizer: People who work within organizations often fit into these two roles. The maintainer has a job to do and does it. We've been indoctrinated into this posture from a young age. Not only individuals but entire industries are charged with the maintenance of systems we depend on.

The optimizer works within a system to improve processes and outputs according to already agreed-upon objectives. If you offer a slightly faster jet, a slightly more efficient cupcake frosting machine, or a slightly better cash register, your improvements will help the system get to where it thinks it wants to go even faster.

232. THE WEATHER REPORT IS A PREDICTION

It's helpful to understand what the future will be like when we get there. But we're terrible at understanding predictions.

If the weather report says that there's an 80% chance of sunshine on Saturday, your wedding day, does that mean it won't rain?

One way to look at a prediction of 80% sunshine is that it's a tug of war between eight people pulling for the sun and only two people pulling for rain. Of course the sun is going to win.

That's not what's happening.

It also doesn't mean that there's a 100% chance it will rain 80% of the day this Saturday.

If the meteorologists have done their job well, what they're saying is that for every 100 Saturdays like this one, in this location, it's quite likely that it will rain on 20 of them.

Here's a deck with five cards in it, one ace and four Jokers. Pick a card at random. The ace means it's raining.

Some people call this probability, which is a five-syllable way of hiding a simple idea.

Probability is nothing but a report on how the deck is stacked.

If we are going to choose our future, it helps to have a hint about what to expect there.

233. THIS MIGHT NOT WORK

The future is unknown. Any project we take on, any change we seek to make, might not work.

We can't do strategy without embracing the knowledge that we're taking a risk.

If you need a guarantee, you'll need the world to stay still. Strategy requires being smart about how we invest our time, money, and assets.

To assist in strategizing we often try to quantify the risk. In that sense strategy is the difficult work of factoring in the unknown to our approach.

Consider that stacked deck of cards.

We're pitching a potential new client, a node in a system that we hope will embrace our new product or service.

How many aces are in the deck? If our pitch goes well, based on our experience and those that came before us, what are the chances we'll get another meeting, or that we'll get a yes?

How much did it cost to get to this moment? What are we risking?

And the systems question: If we get a yes this time, is the next call going to go more easily? Are they dependent events, getting easier as we go, or are we trapped in this loop?

Visualize the cards and you can make smarter choices about which moments, which nodes, which changes, and which systems you're going to focus on.

234. BACK TO THE RHINO

When Dürer made his woodcut of the rhino in 1515, he hadn't seen it in person, or even a reliable first-hand drawing (there were, of course, no cameras). Instead, he made assertions about what he was hearing, piecing together elements of rhino-ness, and would up creating a pastiche of what a rhino might be.

So many prints from the woodcut were made that it became the definitive European image of the animal for centuries to come.

The future sends us reports on what it's going to be like. None of us have seen it, but it's possible to make assertions about what is to come.

We may have to walk away from our drawing tomorrow, no matter how hard it was to create, but the sketching pays off because it offers context and structure for what might come next.

235. WHO CONTROLS THE DICE?

Adam Mastraonni describes the pre-scientific history of man as one in which people were sure that Zeus (or perhaps his daughter, Dike) controlled random events. When people roll the dice, Zeus is controlling the outcome. When a snake bites someone, that's divine retribution. If it rains on your wedding day, that's a sign.

Probability, double-blind medical research, and the scientific method have only been around for a few hundred years. They're all based on the observed fact that systems have a range of predictable outcomes and random events are actually random, not controlled by an unseen powerful force.

There are few divinely ordered snake bites in the Arctic. That's not because Zeus believes that people who live there are morally superior. It's because there aren't many snakes.

No one is controlling the dice, but if we're smart, we can choose a set of dice that are more likely to get us what we seek. Loaded dice and a stacked deck can be found if we look for them.

236. WHO IS WAITING FOR YOU AT THE AIRPORT?

We can't predict the future, but we can get a good sense about what to expect. One way to think about this is to imagine that you're flying to a new city for a conference.

You're told that someone will meet you at the gate to take you to the venue. The group that's meeting you has 20 people on staff, and two of them are very tall.

I'm hoping we can all visualize how this might play out, and what to expect when you arrive.

There's probably a random distribution of who meets which plane, and about one in ten times, a tall person is going to be waiting at the gate.

This probabilistic analysis doesn't say anything at all about you, your skill, the guides, or their approaches—nothing but how your experience might unfold.

237. UNDERSTANDING STATISTICS AND POLLS

If someone says that there's a 90% chance a short person will greet you based on this information, they're giving you a probability. If a tall person shows up, that probability wasn't wrong. It was merely a statement of how many people were in the random hopper and which were tall and which were short.

It's tempting when we hear about polls or probabilities to simply round them up. The chance you won't get dealt an ace in the next card out of the deck is 96%. But it makes no sense to be surprised if you get an ace—you had to get something, and the odds that it wouldn't be any other of the 12 values is exactly the same: 48 out of 52.

There are dice and they are rolled, there are cards and they are shuffled. Random events happen all the time.

Fewer than one in twenty people are admitted into Stanford as undergrads. If you get in, you haven't proven them wrong or beaten the odds—they need to let *someone* in and it was you.

Strategy involves the hard work of looking at probabilities and building likely outcomes into your plans. It might not be in our control, but we can still count the cards.

238. BEST PRACTICES AND THE STATUS QUO

When the world is at rest, a precise instruction manual is a useful tool. Engineers rely on best practices, as does a student eager for an A.

"Do it like this and you will get that."

And for 10,000 years, this is precisely what we did.

We learned to hunt, farm, and fish from others who had already figured out the method. We were trained to work on an assembly line, drive a car, and even paint a portrait.

Best practices reduce our risk and ensure that the dominant system is well-cared for.

Best practices work when we are part of a system, contributing our piece, and living in a world without change.

Best practices turn a blueprint into a guarantee.

But now, best practices are not nearly as useful as they used to be. They can give us reassurance, but they're not always the "best" path.

239. ANALOGIES AND THE PROBLEM WITH "ALMOST"

When the world is changing and we seek to change it, best practices fail. The alternative is to learn by analogy.

In *this* instance, with *these* factors, an approach like this worked. It's almost the same as the one you're confronting.

"But," the careful individual raised on best practices asks, "do you have an example that's exactly like the situation I'm currently in?"

No.

The "almost" is part of the deal.

We have been indoctrinated to seek certainty, go back to normal, celebrate the end of change, seek the right answer and the peace of mind that comes with it.

To find a useful blueprint—an effective strategy—we must seek out analogies.

Understanding an analogy requires we understand the system that makes it relevant.

Once we see the system, we can discern how it's the same (and different) from the one we're facing.

And once we understand a system, we can work within it and we can change it.

---

240. CHEERLEADERS AND COACHES

Who sits at your table? Who has permission to offer you criticism?

Most people are bystanders. They're not the audience you set out to serve, nor are they trusted experts who have the insight and discernment to tell you what you need to hear.

We benefit from finding two types of supporters we can seek out when we're building our strategy.

The first are people who bring enthusiasm and optimism to our journey. We're not asking them for feedback or useful criticism. Instead, they're here to offer encouragement. Cheerleaders cheer. That's their job.

If this is the only group in your life, you're doomed. Your journey becomes a cycle of unfettered "yeses" and you can end up headed in the wrong direction—yessed when you should have been maybe-d or even no-ed.

The other group, the one that successful makers of change can lean on, are individuals who understand strategy. They have domain knowledge, they can ask hard questions, and they're eager to criticize the work (not the worker).

These coaches don't have to have played to be successful. But they need to have seen enough games and called enough plays to have domain expertise and the discernment to understand what plays to call.

They're not always right, but their feedback should be interesting. This group can ask challenging questions that cause you to refine your blueprint.

Today we can train an AI to ask us these hard questions and help us see the path ahead. It doesn't matter if it's a person or not when we're iterating on what's next. It's often the question that matters. *And then what happens?*

241. COLLAPSING TO THE CENTER

Marty Neumeier points out that many brands get boring over time. Systems and feedback loops relentlessly push us to center. It's easier to manage 100 doctors in a healthcare practice if they consistently act in similar ways.

It's hard work to stand for something, stick with a strategy, and to be willing to send customers to someone else for help.

Positioning is a service. It's a beacon to your customers, patients, or constituents. It says, "If you're looking for X, that's what we have. On the other hand, plenty of people are looking for Y, and you'll find that from our colleagues over there."

Positioning isn't competitive. It's the opposite. It turns your competitors into colleagues, folks who do something else for someone else.

But positioning is also a move in a strategic game. When you put yourself over *here* you are also choosing to put people who previously competed with you over *there*.

Some of them will make a move in response. Others will find themselves pushed to the center as you go to the edge.

We need organizations and people in the center, and I don't think we're in any peril of running out of that. But you (and your customers) benefit when you have a strategy to get to the edge you seek to live on.

242. UNDERSTANDING THE 2 X 2 POSITIONING GRID

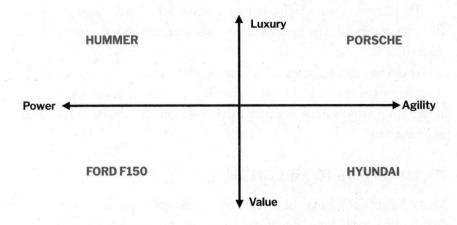

There are two axes, horizontal and vertical. They represent extremes of something that customers care about. They might be safety versus performance, luxury versus bargain, or sustainable versus convenient.

The breakthrough is this: *Each end of the axis has to be something that a customer might want.* Not what you want, what they want.

You can't identify "overpriced" or "poorly designed" as extremes. That's not positioning—that's simply trash talking your competition.

In this sample grid, you can see that any of the four extremes could be seen as reasonable. All four of these cars are the right car for someone, but none is the car for everyone.

Someone who buys a Ferrari or an Android phone or a stinky bleu cheese isn't stupid. They've simply made different choices than someone who buys an electric car, an iPhone, or a cashew-based cheddar.

The magic of positioning is that it respectfully highlights what the choices might be. The extreme ends of each axis might not be something *you* would want, but it must be something *some* people would want.

When you honestly and accurately position the competition, they cease to become your competition, because you sell something that they don't sell.

Bonus: There is usually space to outdo a competitor at what they have chosen to do. You can say that your scarves are more exclusive, expensive, and luxurious than the ones at Hermès, especially if you can back it up. Moving your competition to the center—the catch basin of mediocrity—is a powerful strategy.

Most of the time, though, we're looking for two axes that no one has thought to highlight before. When we find the right combination, we see that one of the four squares in the 2 x 2 grid is wide open, and we can claim it.

In two famous examples, Volvo discovered that the safety/reliability quadrant was empty and filled it. And 7UP distinguished itself from Coke simply by being uncolored. 7UP is not Coke, and proud of it.

Build something that fills a square, and it becomes yours to defend.

A small college without a football team but with plenty of interaction with professors doesn't compete with Florida State or Notre Dame. Instead, it has the chance to be the best option for people who seek that option.

243. THE BLANK OF BLANK

One way to find a successful positioning strategy is to steal one. Go ahead and borrow it.

Shake Shack is the Starbucks of fast food places.

Staples is the Home Depot of office supplies.

The attributes humans care about are from a finite list. People seek out things like luxury or convenience or a bargain. We're not responsible for inventing that list. We simply need to listen to discover what people care about.

Successful positions work because they have empathy for people, not because they represent a universal sort of better.

244. MOVING TO THE MIDDLE (OR NOT)

Positions change as the market does.

Tiffany's built a position for more than 50 years. They were the famous yet exclusive, expensive but not idiosyncratic jeweler for people who wanted to send a message to friends and loved ones.

"There's only one Tiffany's" is very different from "You can buy jewelry from anyone, and we're anyone."

Tiffany's investment in its retail locations, advertising, and package design relentlessly reinforced this position. There was no competitor who could find the resources to challenge them in this area. Over time, earning the right to be called the "Tiffany" of an industry became a genre onto itself.

In 1979, Avon, the mass market seller of cosmetics, bought Tiffany's for about a hundred million dollars. Over the next five years, they worked to change its position—asserting that they were still the top of the line, but lowering prices and broadening distribution. It didn't work, and they wound up selling the brand for about what it cost them.

Sometimes it's possible to move a position successfully down and to the middle, while also maintaining status.

Cheerios has a position of an accessible, low-sugar, and mom-recommended cereal for kids. Healthy and bland.

Honey Nut Cheerios is now one of the top-selling brands of cereal in the US, and they won't mind if you think it shares the same attributes as Cheerios. But it doesn't. It is loaded with sugar and basically candy in a bowl. But moving to the middle and appealing to more people paid off, and they've somehow managed to maintain their reputation.

Shake Shack began as one quirky hamburger stand in New York City. As they've grown in the 20 years to more than 400 outlets, they've maintained their position compared to traditional low-priced burger chains, while also reaching far more people.

Nike went from performance shoes for highly competitive athletes to velour tracksuits for couch potatoes. It won't last forever, but it has certainly paid off—elite athletes are on the payroll, their technology continues to push competition forward, and they also sell low-performance comfort to those that want it at a discount.

245. GOING TO PLACES THE COMPETITION CAN'T GO OR WON'T GO

In many competitive markets, leaders have evolved to serve the widest audience they can. This means that even if they might want to respond to a competitive positioning threat, they may choose not to.

When Netflix pioneered streaming, they released their original shows available all at once, encouraging binge watching. Other TV networks couldn't and wouldn't do this as it worked against their business model, their technology and their culture. "Must See TV" is based on scarcity and time certain, while streaming works on the long tail and any time at all.

McKinsey has billions in revenue, serving any large organization that can afford them. As a result, they've been involved with antisocial projects, including coming up with strategies to help Purdue get people addicted to opioids.

A competitor like BCG or Bain could announce that they are only going to take ethical clients. Hiring them would send a signal. Many clients might choose the benefits that come from being good enough to have a clean consulting firm working for them.

The same opportunity happened after the Enron debacle, and then again with Sam Bankman-Fried. An accounting firm could ask its most questionable clients to move on, and then publicize the fact that they've chosen only to work with clients worth respecting.

Your successful competition stands for something. When you choose to stand for something that contrasts with that, they can't follow you.

246. WHERE IS EVERYONE?

The marketing manager of the new restaurant was earnest, focused, and excited. I asked her, "Who is this place for?"

Her enthusiastic one-word reply: "Everyone."

This is clearly untrue on its face. It wasn't for people from a thousand miles away, or strict vegans, or people who don't go to restaurants, or people who couldn't afford the tab.

But more than that, if it was for everyone, wasn't that equivalent to being for no one?

If they're lucky, 200 people will eat here next week. For the next week, that's exactly who the restaurant is for. They need to create the conditions to delight this group, and create so much positive tension that these early adopters come back and bring their friends.

And then their friends…

You don't need too many doublings before the place is packed full every night. And yet, it will be only a tiny fraction of a percent of everyone.

"Everyone" is shorthand for hope and an unwillingness to see time, systems, and strategies.

"Someone" is far more effective.

247. GETTING THE WORD OUT

When someone shares their marketing frustrations with me, the conversation almost always begins the same way: "How do I get the word out?"

There are many variations. Can you introduce me to someone? Where should we run this ad? We're out of time, so who can I hustle? There must be a shortcut!

And my answers are always the same, in the form of more questions:

- If you don't have time to do it right, when will you have the time to do it over?

- Is this objective really what you want?

- Do your assets match the project you've taken on?

- Why would the nodes in the system you're engaging with care enough to listen to you or take action?

- What will they tell their colleagues and friends?

People with answers to these questions rarely end up with a marketing problem.

248. SCALING BETTER

The easy version of scale is *more*. More employees, more revenue, more links, more press, more followers, more status. For some, this is a kind of better.

But this linear sort of growth only looks in one direction.

There's also the better of emotional labor, well spent.

There's the better of significant system change, of fixing leaks instead of bailing out the boat.

There's the better of creating lasting impact for a few people instead of seeking glancing recognition from the masses.

Can you talk about what sort of better matters to you and the people you serve?

---

249. HALF A BOAT ISN'T MUCH HELP

Don't run out of money, and don't run out of time.

Half a boat will sink. In fact, 99% of a boat is useless. A 100-foot yacht with a 1 foot hole in it is still going to sink, no matter how much you hope it'll float.

To build an asset, we need resources. Time and money are the two most obvious ones.

When we run out of time, we're done.

When we run out of money, we're done.

And if we're done before we've made an impact, the entire effort is wasted.

The scale of your project needs to match your assets. When we take on too big a change, for too many people, we underdeliver, and all is lost.

Back to that boat: If it can effectively carry nine people but not 10, then putting 10 people onboard will cause it to sink. Not only will the last person perish, but everyone involved will suffer.

Each individual we seek to influence will refuse to take action if we have too little to offer. People have choices and they have standards. When we offer something that delivers too little, they won't be activated. Offering a bit too little to a lot of people still gets us nothing.

At every step through time, our project is judged anew. It gains influence, authority, or power, or it flounders.

Living in surplus also creates long-term advantages. Money in the bank compounds, while debt compounds even faster (in the wrong direction). When we extend ourselves beyond our means, we create short-term pressure and a downward spiral if the market doesn't respond on time.

The process is simple but easy to forget: overwhelm the smallest viable audience with a solution that creates the conditions for them to take action.

Repeat.

250. THRASHING AT THE START

Steve McConnell shares the most important lesson about project management: Changing course and exploring your options are far cheaper at the start than they are at the end.

While this is obvious, we almost always do it backward.

It's only toward the end that the boss takes a look, that the community review board gets involved, that we share our idea with the salesforce—because it's at the end that things begin to feel real and imminent, and busy and important and distracted people have trouble paying attention when they have competing emergencies.

The discipline of project management is to insist, "We're not going to write a line of code until you sign off on the storyboards" or "We're not going to lay a brick until the plans are approved."

Once your project launches, it quickly evolves as a result of interactions with the community, the shifts in your insights, and the surprising way time unfolds.

And so a new project begins. Thrash again. At the beginning. Repeat.

251. THE LAST MINUTE

We experience a few kinds of minutes each day:

- The last minute

- The next minute

- And the best minute

The last minute feels like a required part of modern life. We have countless competing priorities, and it's easy to slip into the mode of putting off anything that isn't a crisis off just a bit so we can go back to working on the crisis of the moment.

Of course, the task we put off will marinate for exactly long enough to become a crisis, and then we'll get to it.

Which means that our days are spent in crisis, working on anything and everything only at the last minute.

But time marches on, regardless.

A few seconds from now, we'll be presented with the next last minute.

If we choose, we can spend that next minute working on the task that is right this moment at the last-minute stage of its urgency.

Or we can shift and see projects. We can see projects and we can manage them.

The next minute actually has a chance to become the best minute. Something to be invested and allocated and spent in a way that matches our strategy, not the urgency of those around us.

We can learn to see time and to manage it.

252. EVERY "YES" REQUIRES MANY "NO"S

Opportunity cost is real.

Time is not infinite, and the scarcity of time creates constraints.

There's only a bit of room in your shopping cart. If you have this, you can't have that.

One reason that we avoid choosing a strategy is that we're not comfortable walking away from all the other possible strategies.

Rather than celebrate the paths not taken, we take no path at all.

If you're going to say "yes" to something, be prepared to show us all the things that you would have to say "no" to in order to make room.

Many use social media for three or four hours a day. What could that time have gone toward instead? Is increasing the count of your Twitter followers actually the most useful way to make a change happen?

The question isn't: "How is it going?"

It's: "Compared to what?"

This time, effort, or money you're spending—what could it have gone to instead?

253. EMPATHY FOR THE RETAILER

If they're going to stock your company's new item, that means that they have to take something else off the shelf.

What will they tell their boss?

Shelf space is an asset, and it comes with an opportunity cost. The obvious metric is profit per square foot. The retailer has an insatiable desire to earn more return on the shelves they control.

This means that if you're going to get that shelf space, you'll either need to offer a bigger markup on the same number of sales or more sales per foot.

The system probably isn't open to changing how it sees opportunity cost, so you're going to need to dance with it.

254. BRINGING INTENTION TO PROJECTS

Projects are not simply tasks. All projects:

- Interact with other people

- Have a beginning and an end

- Seek to deliver a desired result

- Have constraints

- Involve unknowns

When we bring intent to our project, we're more likely to avoid drama. And reducing risk is about investing in avoiding problems before they occur.

It's possible to accidentally wander through a project and still have it succeed, but our work is more likely to pay off if we bring intention to the project. We can seek out and dance with the challenges and tension that a project creates, and we can look at each challenge clearly. Like it or not, you have a project culture. What's it like around here?

Can we talk about it? We can begin by announcing that we have a project, describing our strategy, and articulating the change we seek to make.

As Sasha Dichter says, "Tell everyone about your strategy." Tactics shift, but strategies are for the long-haul.

We can identify the people we'll need to work with, the assets we'll need to acquire, and the risks, real and imagined, that the project faces.

Why is this uncomfortable? We've created a cultural bias against talking about building the future. And we've made it worse by avoiding having conversations about the projects that matter to us.

255. SUCCESSFUL PROJECTS

- They aren't static because they move through time and time moves through them.

- They accomplish something.

- They serve systems and enable their participants to get to where they're going.

- They create the conditions for people to spread an idea.

- They create resilient structures that thrive when the world changes.

- They evolve based on useful inputs.

A project is not simply a set of tasks. It's the coordinated work of people engaging with systems, and it has a beginning and an end. There are constraints, assets, and, most of all, time.

Brick by brick, day by day.

Once we see the time axis for every project, our work becomes more clear.

Ahead of us is a dip, a place of difficulty, where most people quit. Our job is to ensure we have sufficient momentum, resources, and energy to get through that dip, because tomorrow is another chance to begin our project again.

Don't run out of time, don't run out of money. Hard decisions now ensure easier decisions tomorrow.

256. THE THREE PROJECT TRAPS

- Communication

- Risk management

- Constraint confusion

On the path from here to there, it's inevitable that things won't go as we expect. Even solo work encounters the unforeseen, but as we add more people, complexity rises.

257. COMMUNICATION WITH INTENT

The larger the team, the more we need to lean into the process of communication. It begins by being clear about our roles, our purpose, the change we seek to make, and the people we're seeking to serve.

More than that, we need to create the conditions for this honest project-focused communication to continually occur without heroic effort. This is how buildings get built and movies get made—when our project culture is obvious and the proxies for progress and quality are clear, the work gets done.

Consider this for a moment: Professional projects have project managers. If it's important, we don't wing it, or hope for the best. Instead, we're thoughtful and intentional about how we talk with each other.

This isn't completed in one meeting. This is the ongoing commitment to creating and maintaining a flow of information over time. The world changes. We're changing it. Without a resilient communications system, the project stalls.

Projects require strategy, but our strategy is directly related to our ability to ship the work.

258. RISKS AREN'T TO BE AVOIDED

The future is an unknown place, and no project is risk-free.

If we say, "Failure is not an option," we've just guaranteed that success can't happen either. Certainty is elusive, and if we require certainty to move forward, we're trapped.

The opportunity isn't to de-risk our work. The opportunity is to see the risks, understand the game, and build our expectations and responses about risk into the project.

Risk is the price we pay to make a difference.

259. CONSTRAINTS ARE A GIFT

"If only" is a soothing refrain. If only the constraints were lifted, and the things that are scarce were abundant. If only the barriers were lifted and there was more time or fewer obstacles.

"If only" is a trap.

If the constraints went away, you'd be playing a totally different game, because your competitors would see their constraints lifted as well.

Constraints are a gift because they bring us something to lean against, and they give us the chance to focus.

Sometimes, the situation changes, and constraints are lifted. In those moments, we need to be hyper-aware of the new possibilities. The rest of the time, instead of cursing the boundaries, we can celebrate them.

The most interesting strategies happen at the edges, and the edges exist because that's where the constraints are.

---

260. WHAT DO YOU MAKE?

- A living
- A time sheet
- Digital buckets of bits
- A widget
- Projects
- A community
- A difference
- Change
- A ruckus
- Choices
- A commitment
- Decisions

Does the way you spend time and money and effort support your answer?

261. PROBLEMS ARE OPPORTUNITIES

When a decision is called for, there must be a problem to solve. If there are no problems, there's no need for projects and no room for growth.

Russ Ackoff's writing about systems asserts that problems have five components:

- A decision-maker
- Elements of the situation that are controllable by the decision-maker

- Elements which are out of the decision-maker's control

- Constraints

- A range of possible outcomes

When all five are present, we get to do our work. The work of making a decision.

If they're not present, then we don't have a problem or a decision to make. We simply have a situation.

Celebrate the problems ahead. Problems are opportunities to create the conditions for better outcomes.

The way forward is simple, but not easy.

First, we need to see the problem. We need to understand the systems, the constraints, and the desires of those we serve. We can become smarter about what assets we control and how we can invest in them and make them work better for us.

Don't focus on a situation, which is not a problem at all. A situation is a mismatch of constraints and goals. A situation becomes a problem when we have the agency to change something and move forward.

Second, we can be honest about our objectives. Almost every inelegant or failed strategy begins with conflicting or muddied objectives.

Then, we can focus on the elements we control as we make decisions. The ones we can't control must be understood, but it's pointless to try to change them. When in doubt, reexamine why you put these elements in the "can't control" category in the first place.

If the project is not working, find a new objective. Make better decisions. Build new assets. And avoid trying to control elements that can't possibly be changed.

Getting stung by a wasp is an unfortunate situation. It hurts. It can't be undone. Other than a bit of first aid, there are no decisions to be made.

Avoiding getting stung by a wasp tomorrow is a problem. We have choices to make, investments of time or effort to consider, and a chance to reconsider the objectives that may have caused the first situation.

262. THE SIMPLE HIERARCHY OF DECISION EFFORT

Our project may require others to decide. The people we seek to serve usually prefer the easier path—and that includes spending less effort on decision-making.

There's a pyramid of decision effort, and unless someone has a good reason, they'd prefer to be at the lowest number, probably level 1:

1. Don't notice, don't care, no decision needed.

2. Think about it and realize our previous instinct was correct.

3. Think about a new situation and make a new decision from scratch.

4. Think about a situation and then make a different choice based on new data.

5. Realize a mistake was made and undo a previous decision.

Each step here is easier than the next one. If your project needs level 5 to happen again and again, that's a heavy lift. People rarely hit the undo button, particularly on expensive decisions, public decisions, or decisions where tribal affiliation is at stake.

This is why it's productive to try to work to move any decisions to the one before it on the list. To help customers or partners reframe what's happening as "We're not undoing a mistake, we're making a new decision based on new information."

This is why it's easier to help someone get what they've always wanted than it is to convert people into wanting what you want.

And this is why real impact comes from building a system where convenience, status quo, and peer pressure push people along in the first category while also supporting your work. If people do a worthy thing out of habit, that worthy thing will happen far more often.

No decision needed is the easiest decision of all.

263. OPTIONALITY AND UNDO

As we dance with the future, we make decisions and investments that intersect with the unknown.

One response is to do nothing. If we can't be sure, better to wait.

A more useful approach is to seek out and embrace optionality. If we can try something, experience something, or launch something that comes with an undo button, that path is far more resilient than irrevocable decisions that can't be undone.

If there's an easy and productive way to backtrack, the best response might be, "Sure, why not?"

Forward motion with optionality doesn't involve stalling when commitments are the better path to make a change happen. Instead, when all other things are similar, choosing the option that gives us more options as the world unfolds is the better choice.

A few simple examples:

When building a spreadsheet, include unpredicted and apparently risky scenarios in your alternative models. You don't have to launch any of them, but it might be useful to understand what the implications are.

When writing a business plan, write three business plans, completely different from each other. You're going to pick one, but first you need to explore the options. In fact, it might pay to write three business plans knowing you're going to pick one at random.

Outfitting a tool chest? Start with pretty good all-purpose tools instead of specialized ones that only do one thing.

If you're planning a flight that requires a connection, choose to connect at an airport that has lots of flights that get near to your destination. That way, if your flight is canceled, you have alternatives.

These all make sense, but how often do we consciously seek out optionality?

"And then what happens?" is most productive when we're okay with multiple answers.

264. GREAT CHOICE, DIDN'T WORK

Annie Duke and Rohan Rajiv have taught me a lot about decision-making.

There's a difference between a good decision and a good outcome.

Strategies start with decision-making and the decisions continue until we reach our goal or realize that we won't be able to. Our decisions improve as we learn more about the systems we're working with, and it's useful to evaluate our past decisions as part of the learning process.

It seems like the best way to do that is to criticize the decisions that didn't work and to celebrate the ones that did. But this approach misses the key insight about decisions.

A decision is a choice. It's based on what we know in the moment.

Buying a lottery ticket is a bad decision. That's because we should know enough about the odds to see that it's a lousy investment. Buy enough lottery tickets and you will go bankrupt.

But if you buy a lottery ticket and actually win the lottery, it feels like you made a good decision. You didn't. You made a bad decision and got lucky—a bad choice with a good outcome.

The flip side is more often true: We correctly understood our options, made a choice, and our strategy didn't succeed.

That's not a bad decision. That's a good decision that was followed by a bad outcome.

Instead of concealing or diminishing these outcomes, we should examine them and even celebrate them. Bad luck isn't a moral failing.

265. HIDDEN DECISIONS GET MOLDY

Smart strategy thrives on explanation and discussion.

Once we realize that a decision is a rational choice based on the available information and our perception of the future, we can see that better information and better perception will lead to better decisions.

A decision is not a democratic election. It's often one person, choosing from available options, based on her risk profile and goals.

But hiding the underpinnings of our decision isn't a resilient path forward and will almost certainly lead to suboptimal choices.

We begin with descriptions about how the world is: "These six things are true."

And then we add assertions about how those facts make a possible future more likely: "And that means that this is likely to happen."

Finally, we describe the probabilities and how our goals and resources intersect with the chances we're taking.

None of these things get better if we keep them private.

Other people might disagree with you about your risk profile or your assertions of the future. And our description of how we see the world is understandably biased.

And yet describing them to people who are rooting for us (and particularly to those that might not be) is a low-cost way to discover how better choices might be available.

The tension and stress of talking about a decision before we make it is real. Yet it's far less than the tension and stress that goes with living with a poor decision we made yesterday.

266. COMPARED TO WHAT?

If someone else had the same information you had, could they have made a better decision?

This is not the same as comparing outcomes after the fact.

Sufficiently complex systems create outcomes that are unpredictable. In the short run, someone will always have a better outcome than expected. They will beat the odds, outperform the stock market, record surprising results, and otherwise appear to be an insightful genius.

For a while.

Warren Buffet lost billions of dollars investing in Dexter Shoe and failed to collect even more by not buying Google stock.

Look closely at any successful strategy, and you'll see bad outcomes occur more often than we would imagine.

Strategies require decisions, and decisions are about the future. Predicting the future in a complex system is an unreliable venture. As a result, unexpected, unpredicted outcomes are the norm.

It's worth calling it what it is: luck.

Resilient strategies accept and account for luck. They benefit from good luck and are resilient enough to survive bad luck.

It's tempting (and lazy) to blame bad decisions for bad outcomes. But they might be unrelated.

267. A QUARTER OF A MILLION DOLLARS

Vanderbilt University is 150 years old. It's ranked as one of the top 100 universities in the United States and tuition is more than $65,000 a year. Counting room and board and other expenses, it easily costs a student and their family $350,000 over the course of a degree.

The University of Buffalo is part of the SUNY system in New York. It's about 160 years old. It regularly ranks as one of the top state schools in the United States. With in-state tuition and a merit scholarship, it's essentially free.

A student who decides that the expensive option is a good idea has a lot of explaining to do. Tuition means that they'll be in debt for decades afterward. Students graduating from the two schools find jobs at about the same rate, and their starting salaries are within $10,000 of each other.

Managing projects begins with the choices we make and the scale of those choices.

We can't do a good job unless we can talk about who it's for and what it's for. We've been indoctrinated to avoid difficult conversations about projects and the money involved, but these conversations are only difficult if we're hiding from the truth of our choices.

If the short-term status of the more famous and luxurious school is worth what it costs, then go for it. But we should be clear about how we make our choices, particularly the momentous ones.

268. THINKING ABOUT MONEY

Many marketers work overtime to confuse us about money. They take advantage of our misunderstanding of the time value of money, our aversion to reading the fine print, our childish need for instant gratification, and most of all our conflicted emotional connection to money.

Confusing customers about money can be quite profitable if that's the sort of work you're willing to do.

A few things to keep in mind:

- The amount of money you have has nothing to do with whether or not you're a good person. Being good with money is a little like being good with cards. People who are good at playing cards aren't better or worse than anyone else—they're simply better at playing crazy eights.

- Money spent on one thing is still the same as money spent on something else. A $500 needless fee on a million-dollar mortgage closing is exactly as much money as a $500 tip at McDonald's (except the latter might change the recipient's life).

- If you borrow money to make money, you've done something magical. On the other hand, if you go into debt to pay your bills or buy something you want but don't need, you've done something short-sighted, and it will extract a toll for a long time to come. Don't be surprised if you discover that many systems depend on us being short-sighted.

- Getting out of debt as fast as you possibly can may be the smartest thing you can do with your money. If you need proof to confirm this, ask anyone with money to show you the math. Hint: Credit card companies are likely to make more profit than any other kind of company in the world.

- There's no difference (in terms of the money you have) between spending money and not earning money, no difference between not-spending money and getting a raise (actually, because of taxes, you're even better off not-spending). If you've got cable TV and a cell phone, you're spending $4,000 a year ($6,000 before taxes).

- If money is an emotional issue for you, you've put your finger on a big part of the problem. No one who is good at building houses has an emotional problem with hammers. Place your emotional problems where they belong, and focus on seeing money as a tool.

- Like many important, professional endeavors, money has its own vocabulary. It won't take you long to learn what opportunity cost, investment, debt, leverage, basis points and sunk costs mean, but it'll be worth your time.

- Never sign a contract or make an investment that you don't understand at least as well as the person on the other side of the transaction.

- If you've got a job, a steady day job, now's the time to figure out a way to earn extra income in your spare time. Freelancing, selling items on Etsy, building a side business—two hundred extra dollars every week for the next twenty years can create peace of mind for a lifetime.

- A small-time investor will almost never get rich by timing the stock market or with other opaque investments.

- The way you feel about giving money to good causes has a lot to do with the way you feel about money.

- Don't get caught confusing money with security. There are lots of ways to build a life that's more secure, starting with the stories you tell yourself, the people you surround yourself with, and the cost of living you embrace. Money is one way to feel more secure, but money alone won't deliver this.

- Rich guys busted for insider trading weren't risking everything to make more money for the security that money can bring. In fact, the very opposite is starkly on display. The insatiable need for more money is directly (and ironically) related to not being clear about what will ultimately bring security. Like many on this path, now they have neither money nor security.

- In our culture, making more money feels like winning, and winning feels like the point. Yet within very wide bands, more money doesn't make people happier. Learning how to think about money, though, usually does.

In the long run, doing work that's important leads to more happiness than doing work that's merely profitable.

269. NO REGRETS AND THE KINDS OF GAMES WE PLAY

The Nash Equilibrium describes the best strategy for a two-player finite game. This is the series of steps that each player should take if they want to maximize their chances of winning given that they have all the information and there are no external forces or luck. Tic Tac Toe has a Nash Equlibrium.

This is the strategy of "no regrets." If we're to play this game, the Nash equilibrium is the best way to play it. Even if we know that we're about to lose this round, it's still the best way to play, each time.

But most of us are not involved in two-player finite games.

Instead, we encounter complex systems, shifting time frames, and different risk profiles.

One approach is to focus on strong links. There are countless factors influencing our decisions, but when we focus on the most direct connections between our actions and the results we seek, we can ignore the emotional trivia that makes simple decisions feel difficult.

Another is to be clear about Maximax vs. Maximin.

Maximax is the strategy of seeking to maximize the impact of your wins. This is the entertainment business, where it doesn't matter if you have occasional flops—what matters is focusing on increasing the scale and impact of your hits.

The alternative is to focus on Maximin. Minimize the impact of your losses. This is the way a power plant works. It's nice if your average productivity goes up a bit, but it's absolutely terrible if something goes wrong and the place melts down.

We tend to default to Maximin, playing it safe and avoiding any short-term losses. But there are places where we should lean into Maximax, being careful not to completely blow it, but embracing small losses as we seek to maximize the benefits of our wins.

This is always a choice. There are very few decisions that offer both.

I was briefly in a friendly weekly poker game. After a few weeks, the organizer suggested I stop coming back. "You're playing to not lose. You make small bets, split the pot, and lower the stakes. But this is poker, not a crossing guard gig."

What's your betting approach?

270. WHY IS IT HARD TO TALK ABOUT DECISIONS?

Unstated instincts, feelings, and desires feel more amorphous and carry less responsibility than the ones we write down and defend.

When we develop a strategy, we embrace the decisions that led to it (and that will follow), and it can be tempting to avoid being clear and engaging with our team.

- We need to explain that we want something and why.

- We need to confront that we might not get it.

- We need to accurately describe the world as it is, which also feels like a judgment on past moments when our understanding of the world wasn't correct.

- We need to announce a specific bet about the future, one that might not happen.

- We need a resilient plan for what happens if the first strategy doesn't succeed.

- We need to be on the hook for following through.

- We have to acknowledge and take responsibility for the potential consequences of our decisions, both positive and negative.

- We need to confront and challenge long-held beliefs, assumptions, or traditions that have influenced past decisions.

- We have to be willing to engage in difficult conversations and potentially face disagreement from others who have different perspectives or priorities.

- We need to be transparent about the decision-making process, which may involve sharing information that was previously kept confidential or acknowledging gaps in knowledge or understanding.

271. BAD LUCK PARALYSIS

The misunderstanding of decision-making in terms of outcomes can cause us to get stuck.

If we get tricked into believing that good decisions always lead to good outcomes, and we can't be sure of the outcome, then good decisions are elusive and we should simply avoid taking action.

It's true that it's easier to do nothing than to feel like we were wrong. But action is our only option.

When we sign up to be a passive bystander, we're ceding our agency and giving up on our opportunity to contribute.

It's impossible to consistently have perfect outcomes. It's easier to imagine that we're able to make good decisions on a regular basis.

A good decision is simply the best analysis of the existing information.

The outcomes can inform our analysis in the future, but the outcomes are out of our control.

Good decisions are worth making, even if they don't always lead to good outcomes.

272. SURVIVORS ARE NOTEWORTHY

Go to a conference of multilevel marketing distributors, NFT creators, or even stock market pickers, and you'll come to the conclusion that these are reliable ways to make a living. After all, everyone in that room is doing pretty well.

But that's simply because the only people who are there are doing pretty well. What you're not seeing are the folks who went broke, burned out, or walked away.

During World War II, a lot of airplanes were shot down. The army hired Abraham Wald to inspect the planes that had made it back to base to suggest how they should increase their armor to improve their odds.

The planes Wald reviewed had bullet holes throughout their wing area. The conventional approach was to add more armor there, where the holes were.

He pointed out the counterintuitive truth: The fact that these planes made it safely home meant that the wings were fine. Put the armor where there weren't holes, because the planes that got shot in the fuselage were the ones that never made it back.

Another example: A company works hard to fix the things that lead customers to call in and complain. That's fine, but it ignores the customers that aren't bothering to call in but who are just walking away or badmouthing you to others.

Figure out what those things are and you'll make an even bigger impact on your long-term success.

The utility of a strategy is not measured by how many people used it successfully. It's measured by what percentage of the folks who used it succeeded.

273. THE REGRESSION TOWARD THE MEAN

Flip a fair coin ten times, and there's a slim chance you'll get ten heads in a row.

The next flip is a 50/50 chance.

The coin doesn't know what it did yesterday. Each flip is an independent event.

But time knows. Time keeps score over the long run. Even though time can't change what the next flip will be, armed with the wisdom it brings, it will accurately forecast that in the long run, fair coin flips are going to even out.

Given enough time, any string of random events will even out.

This is not the same as systems that reward early wins.

When we make decisions, we have to ignore random noise that we call luck, but pay particular attention to systems where winners are rewarded with the conditions that make them more likely to win again.

274. BETTER DECISIONS AND BETTER OUTCOMES

If others are regularly outperforming your strategy, there could be four reasons:

- **They could have a systemic head start**—this sort of luck doesn't even out over time. If the system compounds their initial advantage, it's going to take more than good decisions to overcome this.

- **They could have an asset advantage**—this is a form of head start. A small advantage in assets pays off, they buy more assets, and their lead continues. If the resources and network and skills they bring to bear are to their advantage, you'll need to find a way to find the scaffolding you'll need to replicate their performance.

- **They could have access to better information.** Decisions are based on what you know and how you see the world. If others are seeing more clearly than you do, you'll need to see what they see.

- **They might be better at making decisions than you are.** If all other things are equal, and others are getting better outcomes with the same information and assets, you benefit when you acknowledge that they're better at making decisions than you are—and then learn from what they do.

275. NOT MAKING A DECISION IS THE EASY PATH

Decisions are difficult. There's fear, effort, and risk involved.

As we seek to change the output of the systems we work with, the opportunity is to create the conditions where the decision-makers have an easier time of making better choices. The goal is for it to not feel like a decision at all.

For decades, it wasn't much of a decision for a company like Samsung to send squadrons of people to the Consumer Electronics Show. They made consumer electronics, everyone went, this is what we do.

It's not much of a decision for a lawyer to incorporate his client's company in Delaware. That's what everyone does.

The passive non-decision can be a trap that reinforces negative systemic outputs. The fear of confronting sunk costs can keep us stuck doing the wrong things.

But we can turn these very human instincts to the community's advantage instead.

When all the other doctors in the operating room are scrubbing before surgery, it's not much of a choice. We join them.

If the change you seek to make requires nuanced and brave decisions from people inclined to defend sunk costs, the road ahead is more difficult than it needs to be.

Tamsen Webster points out that people rarely get "believer's remorse." Instead, they will do almost anything to defend their identity and the system they're in.

The most productive thing you can hear from someone you seek to serve is: "Thanks, I was right all along."

We seek to help people achieve their goals, but we do it by changing the way they get there.

276. ASSETS ARE TOOLS

What do you own?

The value of an asset might be what you can sell it for, but it's more useful to see it as a tool that we can use to make something happen.

Some of the assets you may own or have access to:

- Real estate

- Permission to contact customers or prospects

- Data

- A reputation that earns you the benefit of the doubt

- Cash

- Leases with good terms

- Standing (part of the status quo)

- Trained and committed workforce

- Capital

- Intellectual property and trade secrets

- Retail or web traffic

- Hard-earned skills

- Organizational culture

- Licenses and certifications

- Partnerships and alliances

- Customer insights

Assets that disappear when you leave the building are helpful, but the most scalable ones are tools you can leverage by sharing with others.

While some of these assets can easily be acquired for cash, others take time and effort to earn.

Every day, we expend time, and we expend effort. Do you end up with more valuable tools at the end of the day, or have you simply performed tasks for someone else?

277. ASSETS OVER TIME

In 1957, The Rev. Fulton J. Sheen was one of the most famous and trusted men in the United States. His TV slot on Sunday nights was an incredibly valuable asset, and he was able to reach 30 million people every week. For context, there is no show on television today that has that reach.

A friend acquired the rights to all of the old broadcasts. We spent months trying to turn them into something of value, but decades later, his asset value had decreased so much that the tool was essentially useless. The shows weren't as valuable as the time slot.

At the same time that Sheen was at his peak, a small burger stand became McDonald's, and BankAmericard started on the journey that evolved to become Visa.

Each of these assets has gone up in value, day after day, year after year.

What do you own?

278. WHAT SORT OF HAMMER SHOULD YOU BUY?

Professionals obtain assets with intent.

They sell dozens of sorts of hammers at Home Depot. The renter with a new apartment is probably fine with a cheap hammer that seems like it has a comfortable handle. But a roofer or a mason would be disappointed with anything but a purpose-built tool.

Every day we trade time, opportunity and money to obtain assets. If we do this without intent, we'll simply get our tasks done and waste whatever assets we could have earned.

Assets take many forms. What sort of reputation are you earning? Is it resilient, additive, and defensible, or have you settled for being a competent cog in a system that doesn't care that much about you?

After six months or a year or a decade of this work, what will you have to show for it?

The goal is to find assets that increase in value over time, and are resilient enough to transfer to other projects when the world changes.

---

279. COMMUNITY ACTION

The only way to solve a systems problem is with a systems solution.

If there's a powerful system that's industrializing the food supply and processing it in a way that's unhealthy, we're not going to improve public health simply by telling people about it. One documentary about McDonald's is powerless against the powerful systems effects that keep fast food moving forward.

Community action is the boundary that the free market depends on to survive.

Bribery, dishonest labeling, illegal trusts and obvious worker mistreatment are more rare than they used to be. Because of this, it's possible for organizations within systems to behave in a way that feels like a free market to us. These negative behaviors didn't disappear because it was in the short-term interest of competitors to avoid them. They went away because the community came together and made them against the law.

After the standard is established, few want to go back. But there wouldn't be a standard if the community hadn't set one.

The purpose of our culture isn't to enable capitalism. Capitalism is here because it enables us to build the culture we choose to live in.

If culture is the way a system protects itself, community action is the way we push back against culture becoming toxic.

280. THE MAN WHO POISONED US ALL

Thomas Midgely, Jr. invented leaded gasoline. While putting lead in gas made old-fashioned car engines run more smoothly and saved car companies money, it also put lead into the air. The vapors are so dangerous that Midgely himself took an entire year off of work simply to breathe clean air and get the lead out of his system.

Even though he knew of the dangers, Midgely promoted the miracle additive. There was a lot of money to be made, and those that were positioned to make the money embraced his contribution to their system.

Leaded gas didn't go away because car engineers came up with better engines. It went away because governments banned it.

A few years after his gasoline "innovation," Midgely was back. He pioneered CFCs, a magical molecule that could power reliable and efficient refrigerators (for millions of homes, not to mention air conditioners) as well as making aerosols for spray paint and anti-perspirants easier to make.

Unfortunately, each molecule of CFC released into the atmosphere changes the state of thousands of molecules of ozone, the layer of our atmosphere that protects us from direct sunlight, skin cancer, and the boiling of the Antarctic region.

It took a few decades, but the nations of the world got together in Montreal and agreed to a protocol to ban CFCs. And yet, despite the ban, we still have working refrigerators and spray paint. The system figured out how to produce them without CFCs, and the ozone layer is healing, despite the short-term resistance from some people who call themselves defenders of the free market.

Without boundaries, the free market races to the bottom because it finds shortcuts and the competitive system we live with forces many organizations to take those shortcuts.

Actual defenders of the free market understand that the market rests on a foundation. It turns out that community action can raise the bar for all, taking away incentives from people with nothing to lose who seek to race to the bottom.

281. THE ENDURING MYTH OF WIDESPREAD SELF-CONTROL

"If you don't want to smoke, don't smoke."

"If you're worried about lead in your gas, don't buy leaded gas."

"If you are concerned about the environment, compost, recycle, and get an electric car. If everyone did that, we'd be fine."

The system that profits from focusing on mass markets and short-term satisfaction has been indoctrinating us for generations on the moral superiority of individual choice and unfettered markets.

This ignores the power of culture, marketing, and the systems around us.

It also conveniently pretends that there are no long-term side effects to individual actions. The myth that externalities that are hard to see don't count.

We've been pushed to make our circles ever smaller. You're encouraged to worry about just yourself and focus on the right now. This approach is counter to the truth of resilient and generative communities.

The pervasive marketing systems of industrialized cultures are optimized to reduce self-control.

That's what many ads do. They push us to treat ourselves, to find the more convenient solution, and to worry about the long-term later.

Studies show that detoxing from Facebook improves rational thinking and long-term happiness. Yet people still use it.

The price of dog food goes up, but the dogs don't seem any happier. We're happy to buy a story. Promotions and ads work. Systems work. The culture reinforces itself.

We don't know how to change all of the systems that make up our culture, but we can start by establishing standards. Community action creates guardrails, the boundaries that culture needs in order to thrive. Systems crave stability, but stability is impossible without limits—a train without tracks goes nowhere.

We might not need more self-control. Perhaps we need community action.

282. BRINGING A STRATEGIC APPROACH TO THE MOST URGENT SYSTEM CHANGE OF OUR LIFETIMES

Once we begin to see the systems that we live with, the paths to create change become much more clear.

The subtitle of *The Carbon Almanac* is "It's not too late." As John Green wrote, "Despair isn't very productive. That's the problem with it. Like a replicating virus, all despair can make is more of itself."

But how do we get from here to there?

We know what here is. Here is the indisputable, ever-growing body of replicable evidence that shows that the climate is changing. It's changing in ways that will dislocate hundreds of millions of people in only a few years, and change life on the planet forever.

It's easy to despair about this.

Superman's dad, Jor-El, saw that the planet Krypton was unstable and about to explode. But despite his standing as one of the planet's great scientists, he failed to persuade the government to take action. That's how Clark Kent ended up on Earth—and about how almost everyone else on Krypton perished.

We don't live in a comic book, but many who have seen the data and experienced the dismissal, stalling, and opposition of the powerful systems at work feel a similar combination of anger and despair.

Many CEOs understand our prospects, and enlightened government leaders do as well. And yet, pipelines are being built, cattle ranches are being expanded, and some states are banning even wind power.

This is irrational short-term wishful thinking .

But once we see the systems at work, it makes more sense.

Since 1900, the industrialized world has been turning cheap oil into cheap power, without regard for the side effects. That cheap power has enriched 8 billion people and created systems of convenience, comfort, and power that very few are willing to give up.

It's not a hard sell to get someone to switch to renewable power, as long as the power being offered is as reliable, convenient, and even cheaper than what they have now. Power is part of our insatiable desire for more, and offering *more for less* is an easy way to get traction.

That's not a change to the system. That's feeding the system what it's been consuming for generations.

It's clear that there isn't a magic technology that will give us an effortless transition to a reduced-carbon future. Not soon enough.

Are rising sea levels, famines, and suffering what the system wants?

Of course not. But the system is focused on convenience, the status of the players, and the avoidance of the fear of change. Some players in the system see that they can get more of what they seek today even if it deprives others of what they might need tomorrow.

And unlike the solution to the ozone hole, the solution to the larger climate problem feels elusive.

283. HELPING THE MARKET FIX WHAT THE MARKET BROKE

We can now see that systems problems demand systems solutions.

At this moment, our global problem is based on a classic and simple problem in economics: Externalities corrupt the workings of a free market.

If it doesn't cost a factory owner anything to dump crap in the river, they will do it if it saves them a nickel. After all, the effluent goes downstream, away from the polluter.

If it's legal, our culture implies that it's okay. And competitive pressures push producers to take advantage of any externality that saves time or money.

There is a giant externality at work here, one that's so obvious we don't see it: *Each one of us subsidizes the price of carbon, whether we use it or not.*

Jet fuel is sold too cheap. The owner of the jet saves money, and everyone on the planet (and their descendants) pay for it. It's estimated that we subsidized the price of oil products as much as SEVEN TRILLION dollars in 2023.

Beef is sold too cheap. Not only because taxpayers around the world subsidize the production of beef (it's good politics), but because the presence of a billion cows is altering the entire planet. 25% of our impact on the climate comes from the gasses released by cows and the deforestation needed to feed them.

The top ten causes of climate change all exist because they are convenient and cheap, even though in the course of a decade or less, they will create the conditions for disaster, a disaster that won't be convenient or cheap to remedy.

The solution is straightforward but will require community action: *Charge a fair price for carbon.*

The surcharge necessary to end the subsidies can be given back to each citizen in a monthly check, straight to a bank account. The details of this plan are outlined by the Climate Leadership Council, a non-partisan group you can find online.

If someone chooses to fly a private jet to London for lunch, that's a personal choice. Instead of $100,000, the accurate price without a subsidy would be $400,000. The $300,000 surcharge—the part that accounts for all the damage that trip might cost—would be evenly distributed to everyone else.

If we started small, with a minor surcharge and a smaller payment to everyone, very quickly the market would pay attention.

Products and services that embody carbon would gradually go up in price to a fair level. Alternatives would be dramatically cheaper because our personal dividend checks would change how we account for expenses.

The market would more highly value organizations that are prepared for a higher-surcharge future.

Consumers would vote as they usually do, with their dollars. The market might have a chance to solve a problem that a mis-calibrated market caused.

Companies would get what they always seek to get—more sales and more profits. How they do it will change a bit, but no one will have to change what they seek.

We can't shrink our way to greatness. But we can make better decisions with better information.

284. HARNESSING THE INSATIABLE

The power of the carbon surcharge and dividend is that it plugs into the feedback loops and system dynamics that already exist.

Those with an insatiable desire for more money will quickly find a way to sell items that use less carbon, trouncing the competition and gaining market share.

Consumers with an insatiable desire for stability, status, and peace of mind will seek out lower-carbon items, because it saves them money right now.

Once people start getting their dividend payments, a new feedback loop will form. Those that pay attention to embodied carbon when they make purchases will net ever more profit from their dividends. Those that don't care will begin to care.

And no one will have to change what they have always wanted.

If you want to cause system change, find the insatiable desires and connect to them.

285. THE ACTION WE TAKE

It won't matter if you install a heat pump or if you stop using a gas-powered leaf blower.

Well, that's not true—it will matter, except it won't matter enough.

What changes a system is community action. Persistent, consistent, and focused community action.

Find the others, tell the others, organize the others.

And then do it again tomorrow.

Any change worth making requires the focus and persistence to create community action. Systems and culture are far greater forces than any individual can overcome.

Around the world, there are billions of people who are trying to make a difference, but too often, we've been seduced into believing that the only way forward is to do it ourselves. Or wait for someone else to take care of the problem.

The third choice is the useful one. To create the conditions for change. To work together to create community action. Boundaries that amplify the forward motion of the systems that we depend on.

The technology and insights we need to address our climate crisis are already in place. What's not in place is a way to get the market to fix what the market broke.

If we charge a fair price for carbon, people will make new decisions based on new information.

And there are billions of people who want this change to happen, who will benefit from it today as well as tomorrow, and who have the clout to pull it off.

Persistent, leveraged action.

Tell the others.

286. INDOCTRINATION IS REAL

It begins in the delivery room and the nursery.

It continues on the playground.

It is amplified in school.

And cemented at the job interview.

We've been trained to feel helpless when considering the future.

"Will this be on the test?" plus scarcity, forced ranking, pop quizzes, and the endless loop of not quite good enough creates the appearance that we lack agency.

Tomorrow might bring hope, but it probably won't.

Or at least that's what the culture tells us.

Adam Mastroianni wrote, "Today, the primary function of our scientific and educational institutions is to take in young people and lower their ambitions."

We can do better than that.

287. THE JOURNEY, NOT AN EVENT

"I like to leave room for accidents or chaos. Making a seamless record, where every note and syllable is in place and every bass drum is identical, is no trick. Any idiot with the patience and the budget to allow such foolishness can do it. I prefer to work on records that aspire to greater things, like originality, personality and enthusiasm.

If every element of the music and dynamics of a band is controlled by click tracks, computers, automated mixes, gates, samplers and sequencers, then the record may not be incompetent, but it certainly won't be exceptional."

Steve Albini, record producer

The future isn't pre-ordained. But it's also not completely out of our control. The future isn't a labyrinth, or a yellow brick road, or a series of tests.

Can we get it right? Perfectly right? Can we standardize and productize and measure our way to exactly what's next?

The myth of the Industrial Revolution was that we could standardize our way to success. Managers argued that a toaster that was a great toaster in 1963 would remain a great toaster in 1990.

The future is actually many futures, and our future is not impervious to our actions. In fact, our actions (or inactions) are a cause of our future.

And our attitude about the present, the story we tell ourselves about what just happened, is totally in our control.

The game continues, with many players, and it's always new (but it rhymes).

288. CONSTANT PRESSURE AND CHISELING

Labor organizer Saul Alinsky described his most useful systems insight: "... the development of operations that will maintain a constant pressure upon the opposition. It is this unceasing pressure that results in the reactions from the opposition that are essential for the success of the campaign."

Resilient systems evolve to resist short-term pressure. They will seek to outlast you.

And this means that the side with the longest attention span wins. That side is usually the status quo. They have more resources and a history of patiently waiting for the insurgents to lose interest.

Michael Lopp writes about his ability to chisel as a superpower at work. "Once the honeymoon of excitement around a new project is over, most people walk away. Once the system begins to push back, when the status quo seems about to triumph, this is the moment for chiseling."

We chisel when we write computer code or paint, but we can also chisel when we seek to change a system. Not simply our solo chiseling, but organized, persistent, connected chiseling.

A hundred chiselers, doing it every day. Or a thousand.

It's enough.

The change we make with each motion doesn't count as much as the persistence in organizing others to show up and persist in doing the work with us.

We change systems by building our own systems—systems that cause change as their output.

The smart way to address a crisis might not be to dive into addressing the crisis. It might pay to organize people who will consistently and persistently organize people until the system that caused the crisis shifts.

289. COORDINATION FAILURE

An overlooked element of game theory is coordination failure.

When two or more people work together in sync, their force is multiplied.

Soldiers marching across a bridge are trained to walk out of sync, because if they all marched as one, the coordinated force of their footsteps would cause the bridge to collapse.

Of course, if you want to impact a system, this coordination is required.

The internet means that coordination has never been easier. Our ability to find, engage, and learn from each other has never been as great as it is now. Coordination is faster, cheaper, and more open than ever before, and yet we blink.

Coordination fails when we lose patience.

It's not enough to get the right people in the room. And it's not even enough to make sure they're all motivated.

Systems change is a project, and projects respond to leadership and management.

Consider two people setting out to make a difference:

One works overtime to come up with the right answer: "Eureka, here is the solution."

The other organizes and leads a persistent team of people who create a cultural dynamic that others embrace. They start a movement and the movement finds the answer.

Who has a better chance of making an impact?

290. ASYNCHRONICITY IS A SUPERPOWER

Cultures that develop literacy advance faster and further than illiterate ones.

Writing codifies thought and amplifies coordination and persistence.

Writing gives us the chance to keep in sync, even when we're not in the same room at the same time.

We run projects and we make decisions. Both are dependent on our ability to coordinate and communicate with others. We do that with culture and with direct and thoughtful communication.

The coach in the locker room might amp up the team during half-time, but it's the culture that develops from practices, meals, and the playbook that determines whether they're likely to win the next game or make it through the entire season.

Culture defeats motivation. And culture is distributed and rarely happens all at once.

Culture is a system's way of defending itself, and if we're to build a system, we should be mindful of the culture we create.

In our work culture, a distinction needs to be made between meetings and conversations.

Conversations are interactions that share insight and wisdom.

Meetings are real-time memos that waste everyone's time and leave no commonly accepted record behind.

Organizations that struggle with strategy also seem to have a lot of meetings.

---

291. IGNORING SUNK COSTS: A SIMPLE BUT UNCOMFORTABLE IDEA

When making a new decision, we must ignore what we acquired yesterday.

The skills we earned, the machines we purchased, the privileges we were given—they are all gifts to you from the you of yesterday. Like all gifts, they're optional. You don't need to accept them or keep them around.

It's one of the most profound and difficult lessons every MBA is taught: Ignore sunk costs. Money and effort you spent yesterday should have nothing to do with decisions you make tomorrow, because each decision is a new one.

Simple example: You've paid a $10,000 deposit on a machine that makes widgets at a cost of a dollar each. And you've waited a year to get off the waiting list. A few days before it's delivered, a new machine comes on the market, one that's able to make widgets for only a nickel each. The new machine will pay for itself in a few weeks, but if you switch to the new machine, you lose every penny of the deposit you put down, not to mention your time on the waiting list. What should you do?

It's pretty clear that defending the money you already spent is going to cost you a fortune. Ignore the deposit and make a new decision.

Which makes perfect sense until it gets personal. And the work we do, the art we make, it's personal.

You produce a play. A critical scene is your favorite, the hardest to write, the one that you sweated to create and film. But in all the performances you've done, the audience hates this scene, and when you run performances without the scene in place, the buzz is fabulous.

Now, you're not only walking away from a deposit or some training—you're walking away from your best work, from your dreams, from you.

Part of what it means to be a creative artist is to dive willingly into work that might not work. And the other part, the part that's just as important, is to openly admit when you've gone the "wrong" direction, and eagerly walk away, even (and especially) when it's personal.

All effort comes with an opportunity cost, and sometimes that effort turns into an asset. When the asset isn't helping you any longer, you can forgive your effort, decline the asset going forward, and go make the change you signed up for in the first place.

292. WHAT DOES "WRONG" MEAN?

The wrong direction, the wrong answer, the wrong project. What does wrong mean?

Let's go back to where we started.

Who's it for?

What's it for?

If you tell us that you're making this movie for you, your muse, your scrapbook, then whatever you wrote or filmed or edited is exactly right. It's not wrong. Keep it.

But if your strategy is to delight the audience, and the film doesn't do that, it's wrong.

Was going to law school the wrong decision? Well, when you made that decision, what you wanted and the assets you needed seemed clear. Now, five years later, you've learned a great deal and you can see the world differently.

That law degree is a gift from your former self. If it's not going to help you get to where you seek to go, you don't have to accept it. "No thank you." Walk away.

Defending the decision you made to go to law school simply throws more good days after bad ones.

293. TOMORROW IS ANOTHER OPPORTUNITY

There are thirty people over there who are waiting for you to help connect them, lead them, or make things better. But if you're still defending the stuck project over here, the one you put so much into, you won't be able to show up for them.

Customers, partners, clients and students who need your voice or your product aren't going to benefit from it because you're working so hard to dig yourself out of a previous hole, a situation that is now harder than ever to work your way through.

It's easy to focus on the problem right in front of you and to decide that this problem (and only this problem) is the problem that you need to solve. But there's a cost to everything, and the opportunity lost when you're doing this is real, even when you don't notice it.

Of course, we don't create a contribution by flitting from one thing to another whenever things get difficult. But we also sell ourselves short (and harm the people we'd be able to serve) if we're unable to quit a project that's gone sideways.

What happened yesterday already happened. It's a gift and an asset from your previous self. You don't have to accept it if you don't want to.

294. IGNORE SUNK CLOWNS

Yes, there was supposed to be a clown at your birthday party. No, he didn't show up. That's a bummer.

But your friends are all here, and the sun is shining, and you've got cake and a game of pin the tail on the donkey ready to go.

The question is: How long should you mourn the missing clown? How much more of your party are you ready to sacrifice?

The same question confronts the pro golfer who three-putted on the third hole.

Or the accountant who forgot an obvious deduction, one that can't be recovered.

Or the salesperson who missed a key meeting, or the speaker who got let down because the tech crew screwed up her first three slides.

If it doesn't help, why bathe in it?

When we can see these temporary glitches as clowns that are unrelated to the cosmic harmony of the universe or even the next thing that's going to happen to us, they're easier to compartmentalize.

That happened.

Okay, now what?

---

295. WHAT TO WEAR ON WEDNESDAY?

In 1979, it was rare to talk about homosexuality. Millions were trapped in the closet, and homophobia was taken for granted.

Walking on my college campus a few weeks into the semester, I saw some blue signs that people had tacked onto doorways and trees. They said, simply,

"Wednesday
is
Wear Blue Jeans
if You're
Gay Day."

There was nothing else on the poster.

This instantly caused an internal monologue to happen. Not just for me, but for anyone who saw the sign.

What to wear on Wednesday? I don't usually wear jeans—should I wear them in solidarity? What will happen if I'm the only one? Will people judge me?

When thousands of people found themselves asking these questions about identity and cultural power, it began to dawn on many in the community that this was what our gay friends and classmates had to confront every day.

The poster was a tiny step forward on the path of changing expectations and the behavior of people in a system. It began with tension in the head of each person, then turned into conversations among people. It began with someone alone in their room, looking at their closet, knowing that they would soon be among others, in the network, part of the culture, aware that they were about to send a signal.

People like us do things like this.

Tension comes with change the same way shadows come with sunlight.

296. PEOPLE LIKE US

In the State of New York, if a school board budget fails to get a majority of yes votes, the board gets one more try to have it approved by the voters. If it fails a second time, the school is subject to significant cuts that end up impacting students in a negative way.

My little town is proud of its teachers and schools. The elementary school has been awarded blue ribbon status by the US Department of Education, and there's a long history of community support.

A few years ago, rising taxes and shifting demographics led the budget to be defeated. Senior citizens and others who felt less invested in the schools turned out to vote against the budget.

We had one more chance to get it passed.

The obvious approach is to make the argument. To explain to the "no" voters that property values, community cohesion and good citizenship all pushed us to support our schools. To show them that they were wrong and to change their minds.

But time was short, and this sort of argument rarely works.

Instead, three supporters went out and got about 100 yards of blue ribbon. That night, they hung dozens of blue ribbons from the giant tree in the center of town, the one right in front of the high school.

That was it. A symbol. An invitation to participate.

Over the next three days, the ribbons started to spread. Not from the organizers, but by others in town who wanted to contribute. Within a week, there were thousands of blue ribbons on trees around town.

It was a chance to be part of something, to find status and affiliation, and to take action.

The budget passed two to one.

People like us can make a difference.

297. QUESTIONS THAT LEAD TO STRATEGIES

Here are questions worth asking about your project and your strategy:

- Who is this project for? Who is my smallest viable audience?

- What change do I seek to make with this project?

- What is my strategy to make this change happen? Can I articulate it clearly?

- What resources and assets do I have to dedicate to this project? Do I have enough kindling to burn this log?

- What is my timeline for this project? When does it ship and what is my deadline for calling it quits?

- What systems am I currently working within? Does the system want what I have to offer?

- What systems would need to change for my project to succeed? How can I create the conditions for that change?

- Where will I cause tension? What resistance should I anticipate from others (and myself)?

- What are the status roles and affiliations at play?

- How big is my circle of us and circle of now? What can I do to expand them? What about my audience's circles?

- Why would someone talk about or recommend my project to others?

- How can I create the conditions for a network effect to develop around my project?

- Where are the feedback loops, and which ones move my work forward or slow it down?

- Which games are being played? Who sets the rules?

- Which games are winnable, which are oppositional? And which games don't need to be won, simply played?

- What can I learn to increase my odds of success? Where can I gain that knowledge?

- Where is the smallest viable audience? How do they think about status and affiliation?

- Which false proxies are likely to distract me? What matters?

- Am I taking advantage of the shift being caused by a change agent? Or do I need to become one?

- What asset would transform my project? How do I acquire it?

- If an early adopter talks about my project, what will they say?

- Where is the empathy? Does my work align with the actual motivations and interests of the audience?

- What is the tension that I'm eagerly creating in the system by showing up with my change?

- Am I building the scaffolding people will need to adopt and move forward?

- Does this help the dominant forces in the system continue to achieve their goals or does it challenge their status quo?

- What's my position? Are people who choose an alternative making a good choice based on their needs?

- What can I learn from comparable projects that have succeeded or failed?

- Is my strategy simple to describe and hard to stick to?

- What partnerships, alliances or collaborations could increase the scaffolding around this project?

- Am I tapping into an insatiable desire?

- What's the process for altering the strategy based on what I learn?

- Is my strategy resilient enough that we can actually look forward to surprises?

- Is the network effect sufficient to insulate me from a race to the bottom? Can I create a network that is built on abundance, not scarcity?

- Is the change I'm making contagious? How can I alter the culture I'm creating to make it more so?

- How will early successes of my project make later successes more likely?

- What are the tropes and requirements of the genre I've chosen?

- How do we gain insight into the probability that our assertions will work out?

- Can I make it easier for others to decide?

- Where are the non-believers, and how do I avoid them?

- How does my project tap into existing social desires for status, affiliation, and/or security to help propel its adoption and spread?

- What frayed edges, anomalies, or contradictions in the current system could serve as leverage points for introducing my alternative?

- What metrics is the current system optimizing for? How could my strategy re-align incentives and feedback loops around different measures of success?

- How does my project seek to shift part of the culture from a scarcity mindset to an abundance mindset?

- What incumbents might perceive my project as a threat to their power or position? How does my strategy navigate those political dynamics?

- How can I design for network effects, enabling each new participant to create value for all the other participants?

- What sunk costs might prevent potential stakeholders from embracing my approach? How can I lower the perceived switching costs?

- What are the common scripts or objections I expect to encounter? How will I constructively respond to skepticism and resistance?

- How will engaging with my project help people become who they aspire to be? What identity and worldview does it invite them to step into?

- How can I lower the barrier to entry and make it feel easy and irresistible for people to take the first step with my offering? Where is the scaffolding?

- How do I shorten the delay in the relevant feedback loops (or learn to thrive with a longer delay)?

- How do we lower the decision-making barrier to invite participation? Can we make it easy for people to say, "I was right all along"?

- How can I avoid becoming trapped by sunk costs if my initial strategy proves ill-fated? When should I pivot vs. persist? Where's the dip?

- Can I improve project hygiene? What are the standards and conversations I'm avoiding?

- How will I resist the social gravity and "pull to the center" over time as my project matures and faces pressure to conform?

You've always had what you needed to make a difference. But now you can see the systems, understand the games, and ask the questions to turn your project into work with impact. Persistently over time, person by person, day by day.

Go make a ruckus.

298. ACKNOWLEDGMENTS

A few books re-focused my attention on time and systems. I'm indebted to James Gleick for his tireless research and brilliant writing. *Chaos* and *Time Travel* are endless sources of wonder. I can also recommend *Thinking in Systems* by Donella Meadows and the wide range of writings from Russell Ackoff. I wish I had been able to share a stage with both of them.

Annie Duke has been a friend and mentor for years, and her book *Thinking in Bets* is a must read. *Optimal Illusions* by Coco Krumme is eye-opening, and *How Infrastructure Works* by Deb Chachra is a love letter to what we build and what's possible. Jamie Wong has written brilliantly about Thomas Midgley, Jr. The brain trust of Ann Marie Scichili, Simon Sinek, Christina Tosi, and Will Guidara is an oasis of positive magic. Thanks, always, to Brian and Amy.

William Rosenzweig, Derek Sivers, Robert Gehorsam, Rohan Rajiv, Avaleen Morris and Margo Aaron were my first readers, and I made a good choice in having them as friends, co-conspirators, and role models.

Thanks to Steven Pressfield, David Meerman Scott, Tim Ferriss, Kevin Kelly, Arianna Huffington, Lewis Hyde, Bernadette Jiwa, Debbie Millman, Tom Peters, Pema Chodron, Paul McGowan, Chase Jarvis, and so many others who are brave enough to sit down and type. Jodi Spangler is an inspiration and a dear friend. Acar Altinsel gives penguins a good name. Thanks to Madeline, Andrea, Carly, Rose, Don and Nina, and to Dr. Olson Pook! Of course, to Helene, Alex, Sarah and Mo.

Thanks to Becky, John and Julie for doing the work. To David Seuss and Bill Bowman for teaching me strategy.

Thanks to the Purple.space community that workshopped the course based on the book: Saurabh Mithal, Júlio Baptista Barroco, Keith King, kHyal, Molly Brawer, Patrick Smith, Scott Perry, Michael Feeley, Gregory Keyes, Terri Tomoff, Julie Rains, Harris Takas, Wendy Coad, J. Thorn, Joya Mary-Rebecca Jones, Eva Forde, Seulki Chong , Morgane Michael , Jason Taylor, Alford Wayman, Josh Lawton, Jan Black, Bill Tomoff, Mary Ahern, Heat Dziczek, Michi Mathias, Andrea Wade, Jon Titus, Damola Morenikeji,

Diane Alarcon, Joshua Abush, Brenda Ammon, Ric Lindberg, Raymond Weitekamp, William T. Welch, Anat Banin, Annie Parnell, Diane Alarcon, Paul Melrose, Anna Kohler Smith and Lon Wong. Riley Mayer sometimes reads the acknowledgments. Marshall Gans has done important work on the story of self and how we can make change happen, which inspired the riff on the two circles. Thanks to Anne Shepherd, Jacqueline Novogratz, Jim Ziolkowski, Scott Harrison, Jerry Colonna, Ramon Ray and William Reinisch

My publishing career has been shaped by Lisa DiMona, Michael Cader, Stuart Krichevsky, Pam Dorman, John Boswell, Fred Hills, Adrian Zackheim, Megan Casey, and Niki Papadopolous. I'm grateful to each of them for showing me the system and thrilled to join Madeline McIntosh as she helps invent a new one.

Thanks to Jen Shaw, Shana Kennedy, Shawn & Lawren, Skylar, David, Charlotte, Lily, Kira, Chelsea, Alice and a new generation of problem solvers.

The entire GOODBIDS team helped me think through and model how strategy can unfold. Thanks to Jasper Croome, Anne Marie Cruz, Jennifer Myers Chua, Scott Perry, Blessing Abeng, Fani Theofanidou, Claire Aisinger, and the entire team at Viget.

Randall Munroe at XKCD, of course. And Padma Shyam!

This book is dedicated to Niki Armacost, Danielle Butin, Jonathan Sackner Bernstein and to the memory of Wangari Maathai.

A note on AI: I'm grateful for the editorial assistance of Claude, a new kind of large language model. All of this book is written by me, and I'm responsible for its content, but I regularly asked Claude to challenge my thinking. I was particularly pleased with how good it was at completing lists.

At the start of the book, I encouraged you to challenge Claude with prompts and lists from this book, as it's very good at reviewing your work and pointing out what doesn't match the goals you've stated. If you're hesitant about sharing your strategy with your peers, ask Claude first.

PROTIP: IF YOU EVER NEED TO DEFEAT ME, JUST GIVE ME TWO VERY SIMILAR OPTIONS AND UNLIMITED INTERNET ACCESS.

Some other books by Seth Godin

This Is Marketing
The Song of Significance
The Practice
What To Do When It's Your Turn
Linchpin
The Dip
Purple Cow
The Smiley Dictionary

Table of the riffs

BOOKSTORES MATTER

If you purchased this book at a bookstore, thank you.

We have a free gift for you.

Listen to a free bonus hour with the author, Seth Godin, on video or audio, answering frequently asked questions about the ideas in this book.

Visit **seths.blog/bookstoresmatter** for all the details.